First World War
and Army of Occupation
War Diary
France, Belgium and Germany

62 DIVISION
186 Infantry Brigade
Duke of Wellington's (West Riding Regiment)
2/6th Battalion
17 September 1914 - 31 January 1918

WO95/3087/1

The Naval & Military Press Ltd
www.nmarchive.com
Published in association with The National Archives

Published by

The Naval & Military Press Ltd

Unit 10 Ridgewood Industrial Park,

Uckfield, East Sussex,

TN22 5QE England

Tel: +44 (0) 1825 749494

www.naval-military-press.com

www.nmarchive.com

This diary has been reprinted in facsimile from the original. Any imperfections are inevitably reproduced and the quality may fall short of modern type and cartographic standards.

© **Crown Copyright**
Images reproduced by permission of The National Archives, London, England, 2015.

Contents

Document type	Place/Title	Date From	Date To
Heading	WO95/3087-1		
Heading	62nd Division 186th Infy Bde 2-6th Bn Duke of Wellington's Regt 1914 Sep-1918 Jan Disbanded		
Heading	62 Div 186 Bde 2/6 Duke of Wellington W Riding Regt 1914 Sep-1917 Jan		
Heading	War Diary of 2/6th Bn Duke of Wellingtons West Riding Regt. (T.H) From 17th September 1914 To 8th August 1915 Volume 1		
War Diary	Skipton (ref 1/2 Sheet 9)	17/09/1914	08/02/1915
War Diary	Skipton	08/02/1915	02/03/1915
War Diary	Derby	16/03/1915	12/04/1915
War Diary	Doncaster	16/04/1915	18/05/1915
War Diary	Thoresby Park	21/05/1915	06/08/1915
Heading	War Diary of 2/6th Bn Duke of Wellington's West Riding Regt (TH) From 9th August 1915 To 30th November 1915 Volume II		
War Diary	Babworth (Ref 1/2 Sheet 13)	09/08/1915	23/08/1915
War Diary	Babworth	23/08/1915	21/10/1915
War Diary	Gainsborough	08/11/1915	24/11/1915
Heading	War Diary of 2/6th Bn Duke Of Wellingtons West Riding Regiment From 30th November 1915 To January 11th 1917) Volume III		
War Diary	Newcastle Ref 1 Sheet 7	08/12/1915	27/12/1915
War Diary	Newcastle	05/01/1916	06/01/1916
War Diary	Larkhill Camp	17/01/1916	16/05/1916
War Diary	Henham Park Wangford Ref 1 Sheet 88	11/06/1916	23/06/1916
War Diary	Bedford (Ref 1 Sheet 84)	03/11/1916	03/11/1916
War Diary	Bedford	02/12/1916	04/01/1917
Heading	War Diary of the 2/6th Bn Duke of Wellington's West Riding Regt (T.F) From January XIth 1917 To February XXVIIIth 1917 Volume IV		
War Diary	Bedford	10/01/1917	05/02/1917
War Diary	Le Havre	05/02/1917	07/02/1917
War Diary	Belle Eglise	08/02/1917	08/02/1917
War Diary	Louvencourt	08/02/1917	09/02/1917
War Diary	Map Lens 11 E5 C 01 1/100,000	09/02/1917	14/02/1917
War Diary	Mailly Maillet	17/02/1917	17/02/1917
War Diary	Beaumont Hamel	21/02/1917	21/02/1917
War Diary	Bolton Camp	25/02/1917	26/02/1917
War Diary	Point 88	26/02/1917	26/02/1917
War Diary	Artillery Lane	27/02/1917	27/02/1917
War Diary	Safety Trench	01/03/1917	01/03/1917
Heading	War Diary of the 2/6th Bn Duke of Wellington's West Riding Regt (T.F) From March 1st 1917 To March 31st 1917 Vol3		
War Diary	Hawthorn Ridge	03/03/1917	03/03/1917
War Diary	Englcbclmer	09/03/1917	15/03/1917
War Diary	Miraumont	18/03/1917	26/03/1917
War Diary	Logeast Wood	27/03/1917	27/03/1917
War Diary	Englebelmer	12/03/1917	12/03/1917

War Diary	Miraumont	17/03/1917	22/03/1917
War Diary	Englebelmer	04/03/1917	04/03/1917
War Diary	Logeast Wood	27/03/1917	30/03/1917
Heading	War Diary of 2/6th Bn Duke of Wellington's Regt From 1-4-1917 To 30-4-1917 Volume 4		
War Diary	Logeast Wood	01/04/1917	04/04/1917
War Diary	Gommiecourt	05/04/1917	12/04/1917
War Diary	Mory	13/04/1917	13/04/1917
War Diary	Logeast Wood	01/04/1917	01/04/1917
War Diary	Mory	18/04/1917	18/04/1917
War Diary	Logeast Wood	09/04/1917	09/04/1917
War Diary	Mory	18/04/1917	26/04/1917
Heading	War Diary of 2/6th Bn Duke of Wellington's Regt From May 1st 1917 To May 31st 1917 Volume 4		
War Diary	Mory	01/05/1917	02/05/1917
War Diary	Railway Embankment U.26.c.7.0	03/05/1917	03/05/1917
War Diary	Mory B 28a Central	04/05/1917	04/05/1917
War Diary	Railway Embankment U.26.c.7.0	05/05/1917	06/05/1917
War Diary	Mory (B 15d 2.5)	07/05/1917	07/05/1917
War Diary	Mory	10/05/1917	13/05/1917
War Diary	Mory (B.15.d.25)	13/05/1917	13/05/1917
War Diary	Ervillers (B.15.d.2.5) Sheet 57c NW)	20/05/1917	20/05/1917
War Diary	Courcelles (A.15.d Sheet 57c N.W)	21/05/1917	29/05/1917
War Diary	Achiet Le Petit (G.14.a.9.0 Sheet 57c N W)	29/05/1917	29/05/1917
War Diary	Achiet Le Petit	29/05/1917	29/05/1917
Heading	War Diary of 2/6th Bn Duke of Wellington's Regt From June 1st 1917 To June 30th 1917 Volume 5		
War Diary	Achiet Le Petit G 14.a.9.0	01/06/1917	17/06/1917
War Diary	Achiet Le Petit G 14.a.9.0 (Sheet Achiet 57d NE)	22/06/1917	26/06/1917
War Diary	Favreuil (H.10.a.5.b Camp) (57c NW)	27/06/1917	27/06/1917
War Diary	Noreuil (Sheet 57c NW)	28/06/1917	30/06/1917
Heading	War Diary of 2/6th Bn Duke of Wellington's Regt From July 1st 1917 To July 31st 1917 Volume 6		
War Diary	Noreuil (Sheet 57c NW) 1/20000	01/07/1917	06/07/1917
War Diary	Favreuil (Sheet 57c N.W. 1/20000)	13/07/1917	13/07/1917
War Diary	Lagnicourt Sheet 57c NW 1/20000	14/07/1917	21/07/1917
War Diary	Vaulx Vraucourt (Sheet 57c NW 1/20000)	25/07/1917	31/07/1917
Heading	War Diary of 2/6th Bn Duke of Wellington's Regt From Aug 1st 1917 To Aug 31st 1917 Volume 7		
War Diary	Favreuil (Sheet 57c N W 1/20000)	03/08/1917	03/08/1917
War Diary	Noreuil (Sheet 57c N W) 1/20000	04/08/1917	11/08/1917
War Diary	Favreuil (Sheet 57c N W 1/20000)	13/08/1917	20/08/1917
War Diary	Bullecourt (Sheet 51b SW 1/10000)	21/08/1917	28/08/1917
War Diary	Ecoust (Sheet 57c NW)	29/08/1917	31/08/1917
Heading	War Diary of 2/6th Bn Duke of Wellington's Regt From Sept 1st 1917 To Sept 30th 1917 Volume 8		
War Diary	Ecoust (Sheet 57c NW)	01/09/1917	06/09/1917
War Diary	Favreuil Sheet 57c N W	07/09/1917	13/09/1917
War Diary	Noreuil Sheet	14/09/1917	17/09/1917
War Diary	Noreuil Sheet 57c N W	18/09/1917	29/09/1917
War Diary	Favreuil 57c N W	30/09/1917	30/09/1917
Heading	War Diary of 2/6th Bn Duke of Wellington's Regt From Oct 1st 1917 To Oct 31st 1917 Volume 9		
War Diary	Favreuil (Sheet 57c N.W. 1/20000)	01/10/1917	06/10/1917
War Diary	Noreuil Sheet 57c N.W. Sheet 51b S.W 1/20000	08/10/1917	10/10/1917
War Diary	Favreuil (Sheet 57c N.W. 1/20000)	11/10/1917	11/10/1917

Type	Description	Date From	Date To
War Diary	Beaulencourt (Sheet 57c S.W)1/20000	12/10/1917	26/10/1917
War Diary	Gomiecourt Ref Lens II 1/100,000	30/10/1917	30/10/1917
War Diary	Simencourt Ref Lens II 1/100000	31/10/1917	31/10/1917
Operation(al) Order(s)	2/6 Bn. Duke of Wellington's Regt Order No. 38	06/10/1917	06/10/1917
Miscellaneous	2/6 Bn. Duke of Wellington's Regiment	10/10/1917	10/10/1917
Operation(al) Order(s)	2/6th Bn Duke of Wellington's Regt Order No.39	10/10/1917	10/10/1917
Operation(al) Order(s)	2/6th Bn Duke of Wellington's Regt Operation Order No.41	11/10/1917	11/10/1917
Operation(al) Order(s)	2/6th Bn Duke of Wellington's Regt Order No.42	29/10/1917	29/10/1917
Operation(al) Order(s)	2/6th Bn Duke of Wellington's Regt Order No.43	30/10/1917	30/10/1917
Heading	2/6th Duke of Wellington's War Diary October 1917		
Map	Map		
Heading	War Diary of 2/6th Bn Duke of Wellington's Regt From Nov 1st 1917 To Nov 30th 1917 Volume 10		
War Diary	Simencourt Sheet 51c S.E	01/11/1917	12/11/1917
War Diary	Achiet Le Petit Sheet 57c	13/11/1917	16/11/1917
War Diary	Ytres Sheet 57c	17/11/1917	17/11/1917
War Diary	Special Map Moeuvres	18/11/1917	01/12/1917
Heading	War Diary of 2/6th Bn Duke of Wellington's Regt From 1st Dec 1917 To 31st Dec 1917 Volume II		
War Diary	Special Map Moeuvres	02/12/1917	04/12/1917
War Diary	Lens II	05/12/1917	09/12/1917
War Diary	Hazebrouck 5 A	10/12/1917	15/12/1917
Map	Map		
Heading	2/6th Duke of Wellingtons War Diary		
Map	Map		
Heading	2/6 Bn Duke of Wellington's War Diary		
Map	Map		
Heading	2/6 Duke of Wellingtons War Diary		
War Diary	Hazebrouck 5 A	16/12/1917	18/12/1917
War Diary	Lens II	19/12/1917	29/12/1917
Map	Map		
Heading	2/6 Duke of Wellingtons War Diary		
War Diary	Lens II	30/12/1917	31/12/1917
Miscellaneous	A Form Messages And Signals		
Miscellaneous		01/12/1917	01/12/1917
Operation(al) Order(s)	186th Infantry Brigade Operation Order No.69	01/12/1917	01/12/1917
Operation(al) Order(s)	186th Infantry Brigade Operation Order No.70	01/12/1917	01/12/1917
Miscellaneous			
Operation(al) Order(s)	186 Inf Bde Operation Order No.71	03/12/1917	03/12/1917
Miscellaneous	Addendum No.1 To 186 Inf Bde Operation Order No. 71	03/12/1917	03/12/1917
Operation(al) Order(s)	2/6th Bn Duke of Wellington's Regt Order No.7	13/12/1917	13/12/1917
Operation(al) Order(s)	2/6th Bn Duke of Wellington's Regt Order No.48	17/12/1917	17/12/1917
Operation(al) Order(s)	2/6th Bn Duke of Wellington's Regt Order No.49		
Operation(al) Order(s)	2/6th Bn Duke of Wellington's Regt Order No.71	20/12/1917	20/12/1917
Heading	War Diary of 2/6th Bn Duke of Wellingtons Rgt From January 1st 1918 To January 31st 1918 Volume 12		
War Diary	Lens II	01/01/1918	01/01/1918
War Diary	Aubrey Camp G 4 A.2.8 Sheet 51 B	02/01/1918	09/01/1918
War Diary	Special Map Foot Hill 1/20,000	10/01/1918	13/01/1918
War Diary	51 B N. W	14/01/1918	31/01/1918
Miscellaneous	2/6 Bn Duke of Wellington's Regt. Operation Order No. 51	08/01/1917	08/01/1917

(1) 30ε/087 wom

(1) 18ες/οι wom

62ND DIVISION
186TH INFY BDE

2-6TH BN DUKE OF WELLINGTON'S REGT

~~MAR 1917 – JAN 1918~~

1914 SEP – 1918 JAN

DISBANDED

62 DIV
186 BDE

2/6 DUKE OF WELLINGTON
W RIDING REGT

1914 SEP — 1917 JAN

Confidential
War Diary.
of
2/6th Bn. Duke of Wellington's West Riding Regt. (T.F.)

from 17th September 1914 to 8th August 1915

Volume 1

Army Form C. 2118.

WAR DIARY
INTELLIGENCE SUMMARY.
(Erase heading not required.)

Instructions regarding War Diaries and Intelligence Summaries are contained in F. S. Regs., Part II. and the Staff Manual respectively. Title pages will be prepared in manuscript.

Place	Date	Hour	Summary of Events and Information	Remarks and references to Appendices
SKIPTON (REF 1/4" SHEET 9)	17.IX.14		The 6th (Reserve) Battn. of Wellington's West Riding Regiment (T.F.) was created under the command of Bt. Col. & Hon. Col. R.E. WILLIAMSON. V.D. with Captᵉ V.J. BIRKBECK as adjutant, to act as reserve to the 1st line Battⁿ of this regiment. The Headquarters were at the DRILL HALL, SKIPTON.	13.O.I 17.IX.14
ditto.	22.X.14.		96 C.L.L.E. rifles and bayonets were received from A.O.D. YORK.	
ditto.	5.XI.14.		The C.O. congratulated No 2249 Pte. W. BRADLEY, for his courage and prompt behaviour in fitting two men viz. - JOHN SMITH and HARRY ASHTON out of the local canal and who resorted to artificial respiration, succeeding in bringing JOHN SMITH round again.	B.O.40 P+I (5) 5.IX.14.
ditto.	29.I.15.		THE KING was graciously pleased to confer the Territorial Decoration upon Major JAMES MACKILLOP, who is 2ⁿᵈ in Command.	B.O.116 Pt.I (5) 5.II.15.
ditto.	ditto.		The four company organization was adopted.	B.O.110 Pt.I (3a)
ditto.	8.II.15.		The title of this unit was changed to 2/6ᵗʰ Bⁿ. Duke of Wellington's West Riding Regiment (T.F.)	29.I.15.

Army Form C. 2118.

WAR DIARY
INTELLIGENCE SUMMARY.
(Erase heading not required.)

FOLLOWER. I

Place	Date	Hour	Summary of Events and Information	Remarks and references to Appendices
SKIPTON	8.2.15		"C" Company of this unit proceeded on detachment to form part of the Composite 1/2 Battalion. of this Unit and the 2/7 West Riding Regiment (T.F.) at WITHERNSEA (at 1" sheet 33) for the purpose of Coast defence. Major J. MACKILLOP T.D. being in Command thereof, (and subsequently Capt. W. CLAUGHTON)	J.M.M.
do.	2.III.15.		Until this date, with the exception of the above-mentioned move, the Battalion was billetted in SKIPTON and neighbourhood and proceeded with its initial Company & Battalion training and also to obtain as many recruits as possible, holding recruit meetings & going on recruit marches continuously in the area, but then proceeded to join the 2/2nd WEST RIDING INFANTRY BRIGADE under the command of Bt. Col. H.G. MAINWARING at DERBY (at ½" sheet 17.) where the unit was billetted. From time to time officers, NCOs & men were vaccinated and inoculated & small detachments strength about 15 and interchanged with the 1st. line Unit.	J.M.M.

Army Form C. 2118.

WAR DIARY
or
INTELLIGENCE SUMMARY.
(Erase heading not required.)

FOLLOWER II

Place	Date	Hour	Summary of Events and Information	Remarks and references to Appendices
DERBY.	16.III.15		From this date the Battalion will be shewn in the General Monthly Returns as laid down in Northern Command Order, in lieu of that set out in M.R.	N.C.O. & Men 375. Officers 10.15.
ditto.	31.III.15		The date 96 C.L.L.E. rifles and bayonets were returned to A.O.D. YORK.	ditto.
ditto.	5.IV.15		Captn G. H. ERMEN appointed Adjutant from 3rd inst. vice Capt. V. J. BIRKBECK sick leave.	B.O. 166 App. T(a) 5.4.15.
ditto.	9.IV.15		200 C.L.L.E. rifles and bayonets were received from A.O.D. YORK.	ditto.
ditto.	2.IV.15 to 12.IV.15		The battalion continued training under Supervision of its Brigade.	ditto.
ditto.	12.IV.15		On this date the battalion moved to DONCASTER (ref ½" sheet 13) and were under canvas for the first time, being encamped on the racecourse there.	ditto.
DONCASTER	16.IV.15		850 Japanese Rifles and bayonets were issued to the Battalion.	ditto.
ditto.	24.IV.15		1000 sets of Equipment (Pattern 1914) were received, which in effect the battalion became fully equipped, as it had long been held clothing & small kit.	ditto.

Army Form C. 2118.

WAR DIARY
or
INTELLIGENCE SUMMARY.
(Erase heading not required.)

FOLLOWER III

Place	Date	Hour	Summary of Events and Information	Remarks and references to Appendices
DONCASTER	4.V.15		Capt. & Adjt. G. HERMEN after a short illness died at his residence GARGRAVE.	B.O. 198. A.G. 13.VI.15
ditto	ditto		262 N.C.Os and men proceeded to SKIPTON and were transferred to the 3rd line unit.	B.O. 196. A.G. 11.VI.15
ditto	11.V.15		4 Officers and 130 N.C.Os & men proceeded to SKIPTON and were transferred to the 3rd line unit.	ditto
ditto	do.		100 setts of Mills' Web Equipment Pattern '08 were received.	ditto
ditto	13.V.15	9 p.m.	"C" Company rejoined the Battalion after fulfilling its Coast defence duties.	ditto
ditto	14.V.15		The said 200 C.L.L.E. Rifles & bayonets were returned to A.O.D. YORK.	ditto
ditto	15.V.15		2 Officers and 233 N.C.Os men were transferred to 2nd Coast Battalion.	S.B.O. 207. A.G. II.(5) 29.VI.15
ditto	ditto		30 Japanese rifles and bayonets were handed over to 2/2 W.R.I.B.	ditto
ditto	16.V.15	8 a.m.	The Battalion marched to THORESBY PARK (ref. 1" sheet 46) where it took up its new encampment along with other units of its brigade, after having first proceeded with its training in drill &c., with the exception that machine gun & transport returns were formed.	ditto

Army Form C. 2118.

WAR DIARY
INTELLIGENCE SUMMARY
(Erase heading not required.)

FOLLOWER IV

Place	Date	Hour	Summary of Events and Information	Remarks and references to Appendices
THORESBY PARK.	21.V.15		101 Japanese Rifles & bayonets were handed over to the 1st COAST BATTALION.	Sgd. [illeg] B.O. 212 [illeg]
ditto.	8.VI.15		The battalion machine Gun section was completed.	Sgd. [illeg]
ditto.	16.VI.15		149 Japanese Rifles & bayonets were handed over to the 2/3 BRIGADE. Sgd. [illeg]	Sgd. [illeg]
ditto.	17.VI.15		The Regimental Signalling sections were constituted. The Battalion Signalling Section comprising 1 Sgt, 1 Cpl, & 16 men. do. 1 N.C.O. & 8 men.	B.O. 237. A.F.T.(4) 7/1/15 B.O. 238 A.F.T.(4) 30 W/15 B.O. 222.8 Pt. I(3) Pt. I(8) 18.VI.15
ditto.	17.VI.15		A bunale bullay "NIGGER" was taken on the strength of Regimental Amount being the gift of J.H. Deavers Esq. Dunkope. 20 Japanese Rifles & bayonets were handed over to the 2/3 BRIGADE.	Sgd. [illeg] B.O. 225 Sgd. [illeg] Pt.1.(3) 22.VI.15
ditto.	18.VI.15		Capt. N.A. ENGLAND appointed Adjutant from 5th. ult.	Sgd. [illeg] B.O. 235.
ditto.	20.VI.15		63 N.C.Os & men transferred to 27th. PROVISIONAL BATTN.	Sgd. [illeg] P.I(3) 22.VI.15
ditto.	26.VI.15		A draft consisting of 186 N.C.Os & men proceeded from the BRITISH EXPEDITIONARY FORCE in FRANCE.	B.O. 237. Sgd. [illeg] Pt.I.(1) 29.VI.15
ditto.	28.VI.15		200 sets of Mills Webb & Equipment Pattern 08 received.	Sgd. [illeg]

Army Form C. 2118.

WAR DIARY
~~INTELLIGENCE SUMMARY~~.
(Erase heading not required.)

FOLLOWER. V

Place	Date	Hour	Summary of Events and Information	Remarks and references to Appendices
THORESBY PARK.	3.VII.15.		200 sets of Mili' Webb Equipment Pattern 08 were received	Pivot Gun.
ditto.	6.VII.15.		300 ditto.	
ditto.	6.VIII.15.		Up to this date the Battalion has undergone its training as hitherto, but in addition Snipers & Lewis gun operators were commenced at this station, when it marched to BABWORTH (ref ½" sheet 13) where it encamped together with the 2/5 Bt⁰ WEST RIDING REGMNT. under supervision of their BRIGADE.	GWO

Confidential.
War Diary

of

2/6th Bn Duke of Wellingtons West Riding Regt (T.F.)

from 9th August 1915 to 30th November 1915

Volume II

Army Form C. 2118.

WAR DIARY
or
INTELLIGENCE SUMMARY.
(Erase heading not required.)

Instructions regarding War Diaries and Intelligence Summaries are contained in F.S. Regs., Part II. and the Staff Manual respectively. Title pages will be prepared in manuscript.

Place	Date	Hour	Summary of Events and Information	Remarks and references to Appendices
BARWORTH (nf "½" SHEET 13)	9.8.15.		2 Officers & 101 N.C.Os & men transferred from 3rd line Unit and taken on the strength.	B.O. 271 Pt II (6) 9.8.15
ditto.	16.8.15.		200 old Mills belt Equipment Pattern '08 received from Ordnance, York.	
ditto.	17.8.15.		The Grenadier Section was formed comprising 1 Officer 58 N.C.Os & men.	B.O. 278 Pt I (7) 17.8.15
ditto.	18.8.15.		Capt. R.B. CAMPBELL, Superintendent Gymnasia, Northern Command delivered a lecture on Physical Training and Bayonet Fighting to all Officers and N.C.Os.	B.O. 278 Pt I (3) 17.8.15
ditto.	20.8.15.		The remaining 150 sets of Equipment (Pattern 1914) on charge were returned to Ordnance York.	
ditto.	21.8.15.		The Scout Section was formed comprising 1 Officer 20 N.C.Os & men.	B.O. 282 Pt I (4) 21.8.15
ditto.	23.8.15.		Lt. Col. & Hon. Col. R.E. WILLIAMSON V.D. being temporarily disabled by reason of an accidental fracture this left by Major W. CLAUGHTON taking over temporary command during the former's absence.	B.O. 283 Pt I (6) 23.8.15

1577 Wt. W10791/1773 500,000 1/15 D. D. & L. A.D.S.S./Forms/C. 2118.

Army Form C. 2118.

WAR DIARY
or
INTELLIGENCE SUMMARY.
(Erase heading not required.)

Yillers I

Place	Date	Hour	Summary of Events and Information	Remarks and references to Appendices
BABWORTH.	23.8.15.		Professor SMITHELLS (keen humoring) delivered a lecture to all officers, 200 NCOs + men + attached R.A.M.C. on Poisonous Gases.	(B.D. 365 Pat. (7) 23.8.15
ditto	25.8.15		The transport section was complete & had in charge the following:— 10 Riding Horses— 8 H.D. Horses— 13 L.D. Horses— 21 L.D. Mules— 9 Pack Mules— 4 Field Kitchens— Maltese Cart. 2 Water Carts— 2 G.S. Limber Wagons (S.A.A) 5 do. (S.A.A) 1 do. (M.G) 1 do. (M.G. S.A.A)	
ditto	26.8.15		25 Japanese rifles, bathroom & bayonets were returned to Ordnance Yard.	
ditto	3.9.15.		45 ditto & lecture on charge, received from O/C 2/4 Br West Riding Regiment	

Army Form C. 2118.

WAR DIARY
or
INTELLIGENCE SUMMARY.

(Erase heading not required.)

Instructions regarding War Diaries and Intelligence Summaries are contained in F.S. Regs., Part II. and the Staff Manual respectively. Title pages will be prepared in manuscript.

FOLLOWER II

Place	Date	Hour	Summary of Events and Information	Remarks and references to Appendices
BABWORTH	13.IX.15		2/Lieut H.H. RISHWORTH died as a result of a motor cycle accident	{B.O. 306 Pt II (1) 18.IX.15
ditto	14.IX.15		Col. W. OLIVER MOSSE took over the command of the battalion	{B.O. 302 Pt II (6) 14.IX.15
ditto	23.IX.15		11 Japanese Rifles Pattern 1907 bayonets were received from Ordnance & taken on charge.	
ditto	25.IX.15		B.O. 302 Pt II (1) 14.IX.15 relating to the command of Col. W. OLIVER MOSSE was cancelled	{B.O. 312 Pt II (1) 25.IX.15
ditto	26.IX.15		14 Japanese Rifles Pattern 1907 bayonets were returned to Ordnance	
ditto	27.IX.15		29 Recruits were taken on strength -	{B.O. 313 Pt II (4) 27.IX.15
ditto	29.IX.15		14 Japanese Rifles Pattern 1907 bayonets were returned to Ordnance.	
ditto	1.X.15		Major JAMES MACKILLOP T.D. took over the command of the battalion	{B.O. 317 Pt II (1) 1.X.15
ditto	18.X.15		85 Japanese Rifles Pattern 1907 bayonets were received from 186th INFANTRY BRIGADE and taken on charge	

WAR DIARY
or
INTELLIGENCE SUMMARY

Army Form C. 2118.

FOLLOWER VII

Place	Date	Hour	Summary of Events and Information	Remarks and references to Appendices
BABWORTH	2.X.15		Up to this date the Battalion pursued its training as hitherto - Field and Brigade operations and musketry and being also carried out and also after initial training the Japanese musketry Course was fired at TOTLEY RANGE, near SHEFFIELD (nt ½" SHEET 13). A detachment of Officers and 100 N.C.O.s & men joined the BRIGADE RECRUITING COLUMN for four weeks and amongst other operated in the Battalion's own districts. 43 recruits were obtained for the unit. The MINISTER OF MUNITIONS REPRESENTATIVE examined and accepted 34 N.C.O.s & men for munitions work.	(B.O. 333) Pt II (1) (4) (20. X. 15")
GAINSBOROUGH	6.XI.15		On this date the Battalion marched to GAINSBOROUGH (nt ½" SHEET 13) where it took up its winter quarters - no longer being under Canvas - 34 N.C.O.s & men transferred to 24th PROVISIONAL BATN & others of strength accordingly.	(B.O. 347) Pt II (1) 5-XI-15" War Office letter 6.XI.15 of General No 3449 (A.G.1)
ditto	15.XI.15		The establishment of N.C.O.s & men temporarily reduced to 600	B.O. 356 Pt II (3) 15. XI. 15
ditto	17.XI.15		103 men transferred to 3/6 Bn WEST RIDING REGIMENT and struck off the strength accordingly.	

Army Form C. 2118.

WAR DIARY
or
~~INTELLIGENCE SUMMARY.~~
(Erase heading not required.)

FOLLOWER IV

Place	Date	Hour	Summary of Events and Information	Remarks and references to Appendices
GAINSBOROUGH	19.XI.15		21 N.C.Os + men transferred to 26th PROVISIONAL BATTALION and struck off the strength.	B.O. 318 Pgh (1) 19.XI.15
ditto.	22.XI.15		The 9 hired horses on charge were returned to Ordnance in exchange for which 9 G.S. wagons were received and taken on charge.	
ditto.	24.XI.15		Up to this date the Battalion continued its training at Kirkton. On this date it moved to NEWCASTLE-UPON-TYNE (of "SHEET 7") by train + train load of horses — but the exception of clothing, equipment and rifles all ordnance stores held in charge has been handed over to the 2/5" YORKSHIRE REGMNT. in exchange for similar stores held by them, with which REGMNT. inventories were also exchanged. —	Supplemental 24.11.15 filed with B.Os.

Duplicate.

Confidential
War Diary.
of
2/6th Bn Duke of Wellington's West Riding Regiment.

(T.F.)

from 30th November 1915, to ~~31st January. 1916.~~ 30th June 1916. January 11th 1917

Volume. III.

Army Form C. 2118.

WAR DIARY
or
INTELLIGENCE SUMMARY.
(Erase heading not required.)

Instructions regarding War Diaries and Intelligence Summaries are contained in F.S. Regs., Part II. and the Staff Manual respectively. Title pages will be prepared in manuscript.

Place	Date	Hour	Summary of Events and Information	Remarks and references to Appendices
NEWCASTLE of 1st Bat 7.	8-12-15		CHIEF INSPECTOR QR MR SERVICES inspected the REGIMENTAL TRANSPORT on the TOWN MOOR.	See.
ditto	9-12-15		BRIGADIER GENERAL F.F. HILL C.B. D.S.O. took over the command of the 186th INFANTRY BRIGADE vice COLONEL MAINWARING resigned.	See Div Order Juno 1217. 11-12-15
ditto	9-12-15		THE ASSISTANT SUPERINTENDENT of GYMNASIA N.C. inspected the physical training	See B.O. 374 Pt 1(ii) 8.12.15
ditto	17-12-15		BRIGADIER GENERAL F.F. HILL C.B. D.S.O inspected the BATTALION.	See.
ditto	20-12-15		A GUARD of HONOR comprising 3 Officers and 100 N.C.O.'s men paraded in connection with the presentation of a captured German gun to the LORD MAYOR & CITIZENS of NEWCASTLE and a letter of appreciation from BRIGADIER GENERAL MONTGOMERIE Commanding the Tyne Garrison was received therefor.	B.O. 382. Pt 1(3) 21.12.15 B.O. 388 ditto 23.12.15 Jun.
ditto	27-12-15		MAJOR JAMES MACKILLOP T.D. proceeded to FRANCE on a course of Instruction and MAJOR W. CLAUGHTON took over the command during his absence	B.O. 391 Juno Pt 1(iv) 27.12.15

T2134. Wt. W708—776. 500000. 4/16. Sir J. C. & S.

Army Form C. 2118.

39.

WAR DIARY
or
INTELLIGENCE SUMMARY.
(Erase heading not required.)

FULLOWER I

Place	Date	Hour	Summary of Events and Information	Remarks and references to Appendices
NEWCASTLE	5.1.16		MAJOR JAMES MACKILLOP T.D. having returned from FRANCE takes over the command	B.O. 4 Part I (3) 5.1.16
ditto	6.1.16		After having continued its training as heretofore on this date the battalion moves to LARKHILL CAMP, SALISBURY PLAIN (ref Scale 1" O.S. SALISBURY PLAIN) by train and then left w/o its guards in the hut tent Camp. After having handed over all surplus Ordnance Stores held in charge to the 28th PROVISIONAL BATTALION.	Part I
LARKHILL CAMP	17.1.16		GENERAL the RIGHT HON. SIR A.H. PAGET G.C.B. K.C.V.O. commanding Salisbury Training Centre inspected the battalion, being the one selected from the 186th INFANTRY BRIGADE for the inspection	Part I
ditto	20.1.16		180 men were transferred from 3/6th Bn. WEST RIDING REGT and taken on the strength of the battalion.	B.O. 15 Part I (1) 20.1.16
ditto	20.1.16		100 rifles short M.L.E. III* afflies H.V.A. normal sights together with the like numbers of oil bottles, pullthroughs, sword bayonets/07 and scabbards/07 taken on charge.	

Army Form C. 2118.

WAR DIARY
or
INTELLIGENCE SUMMARY.
(Erase heading not required.)

FOLLOWER II

Place	Date	Hour	Summary of Events and Information	Remarks and references to Appendices
LARKHILL CAMP	12/1/16		Previous scale of expenditure of 22 minutes ammunition cancelled. New scale:— 95 rounds per man per month.	B.O. 15 P4 (12). Reg
ditto	25/1/16		1 LEWIS MACHINE GUN taken on charge of battalion.	
ditto	28/1/16		Authority given for increase of number of Corporals in battalion by 2 per company. the number of pver L/Cpls in battalion to be reduced by 8 accordingly. Reg	B.O. 22 P4 (11)
ditto	31/1/16		Battalion was inspected by VISCOUNT FRENCH. He expressed his appreciation of the steadiness under arms and smart soldierly appearance of all ranks. Reg	B.O. 24 P4 (11) B.O. 26 P4 (14)
ditto	3/2/16		62 men retransferred to 3/6 BN WEST RIDING REGT	Reg B.O. 25 P4 (11)
ditto	14/2/16		Henceforth the Battalion will be known as the 3/6 BN. DUKE OF WELLINGTON'S REGT.	Reg B.O. 37 P4 (16)
ditto	14/2/16		46 men transferred from 16/2/16 to the 27th PROV. BATT.	Reg B.O. 37 P4 (15)
ditto	15/2/16		Lt Col R.E. WILLIAMSON resumed his command on 10/2/16	Reg B.O. 38 P4 (14)

T2134. Wt. W708—776. 500000. 4/15. Sir J. C. & S.

Army Form C. 2118.

WAR DIARY
or
INTELLIGENCE SUMMARY.
(Erase heading not required.)

FOLLOWER III

Instructions regarding War Diaries and Intelligence Summaries are contained in F.S. Regs., Part II. and the Staff Manual respectively. Title pages will be prepared in manuscript.

Place	Date	Hour	Summary of Events and Information	Remarks and references to Appendices
LARKHILL CAMP	10/2/16		Transport Officer congratulated by G.O.C. 186th INFANTRY BRIGADE on satisfactory report received from A.D.V.S. on inspection of horses and mules on 14/2/16.	B.O. 39 P.H.(4)
ditto	15/2/16		Battalion Sniping Section formed. Strength — 1 officer, 20 men.	B.O. 41 P.H.(17)
ditto	19/2/16		21 men transferred here from 3/6 Bn DUKE OF WELLINGTON'S REGT	R.O. 42 P.H.III.
ditto	22/2/16		LIEUT. J.W. WOODHEAD ceased to be attached to this unit from 3/6 Bn. DUKE OF WELLINGTON'S REGT from 7/2/16.	B.O. 44 P.H.(1)
ditto	22/2/16		CAPT. N. CLAPHAM transferred to 27th Prov. Batt. from 22/2/16.	B.O. 44 P.H.(11)
ditto	22/2/16		MAJOR JAMES MacKILLOP gazetted temporary LIEUT-COLONEL, dated 30/9/15	R.O. 45 P.H.(13)
ditto	1/3/16		11 men transferred from this unit to 27th PROV. BATT. under date 27/2/16.	B.O. 46 P.H.(1)
ditto	4/3/16		3 LEWIS MACHINE GUNS complete taken on charge.	R.O.

Army Form C. 2118.

WAR DIARY
or
INTELLIGENCE SUMMARY.
(Erase heading not required.)

FOLLOWER IV

Place	Date	Hour	Summary of Events and Information.	Remarks and references to Appendices
LARKHILL CAMP.	4/3/16		2/Lt. A. SOMERVELL gazetted temporary LIEUTENANT with time 5.1.16.	B.O 59 Pt/4(7) KM
do	6/3/16 to 30/3/16		360 Recruits from Army Reserve Class B taken on the strength of the Battalion. 35 of these were subsequently struck off the strength and transferred to Home Service Units or returned to Class B Army Reserve.	B.O 60 Pt/4(6) KM
do	11/3/16		Lieut A.E. BOOTH appointed temporarily in command of letter "C" Company as from 4/11/15.	B.O 71 Pt/4(6) KM
do	27/3/16		2/Lt R. O'NEILL appointed Supervising Officer of Battalion Recruits	B.O 71 Pt/4(6) KM
do	27/3/16 and 30/3/16		G.O.C. DIVISION inspected all Recruits, Army Reserve Class B.	{ B.O 71 Pt/4(5) and B.O 72 Pt/4(6) } KM
do	29/3/16		2/Lt R.M. WIMBUSH and 2/Lt J. NIGHTINGALE transferred to this unit from 3rd LINE and posted to "B" COMPANY.	B.O 75/4/4(4) KM

Army Form C. 2118.

WAR DIARY
or
INTELLIGENCE SUMMARY.
(Erase heading not required.)

FOLLOWING WEEK

Instructions regarding War Diaries and Intelligence Summaries are contained in F. S. Regs., Part II. and the Staff Manual respectively. Title pages will be prepared in manuscript.

Place	Date	Hour	Summary of Events and Information	Remarks and references to Appendices
LARKHILL CAMP.	24/3/16		MAJOR N.A. ENGLAND qualified and passed 1st CLASS DISTINGUISHED as a Rifle Course R.A.I	A.O. 74 P.H. (6) S.C.T. (item 55)
do.	28/3/16		400 RIFLES SHORT M.L.E. III* with all bottles, pull-throughs, sword bayonets and scabbards taken on charge R.A.I	
do.	3/4/16		Henceforth men trained in use of hand grenades will be known as "BOMBERS" M.H	B.O. 83 P.H. (6)
do.	6/4/16		A.D.V.S. inspected the horses and stables of the Battalion. R.A.I	R.O. 5 14.16
do.	8/4/16		CAPTAIN S.P. ASHLEY relinquished his commission on account of ill-health, under date 3/4/16 R.O.I	B.O. 89 P.H. (6)
do.	21/4/16		2/2 WEST RIDING F.A. BRIGADE affiliated to 186th INFANTRY BRIGADE for training purposes. R.O.I	B.O. 97 P.H. (6)
do.	22/4/16		2/Lt T. NIGHTINGALE appointed ASSISTANT MUSKETRY OFFICER. R.O.I	B.O. 98 P.H. (6)

Army Form C. 2118.

WAR DIARY
or
INTELLIGENCE SUMMARY.
(Erase heading not required.)

FOLLOWER 47

Instructions regarding War Diaries and Intelligence Summaries are contained in F. S. Regs., Part II. and the Staff Manual respectively. Title pages will be prepared in manuscript.

Place	Date	Hour	Summary of Events and Information	Remarks and references to Appendices
LARKHILL CAMP	13/5/16		Battalion team won DIVISIONAL FIVE MILE CROSS COUNTRY RUN, organised by SOUTHERN COS. CROSS COUNTRY ASSN	LARKHILL 102. Ref.
do.	15/5/16 to 19/5/16		The Battalion carried out a Military Regiment, marching to PEWSEY, DEVIZES, TROWBRIDGE, MARKET LAVINGTON and thence back to LARKHILL. Billets were occupied at the places mentioned.	A.9.123. Ref.
do.	14/5/16		2/LIEUT C.G.C. KILNER promoted temp. LIEUT. under A.O. 74.XX.1915	Ref. A.9.120. Pages 31-16
do.	4/5/16		2/LIEUT J.A. COLLINGE promoted temp. LIEUT under A.O. Sept Q. 1915	Ref. do. do.
do.	14/5/16		Temp LIEUT A.E. BOOTH promoted temp. CAPTAIN under A.O.R. 12/2/15	Ref. A.Q.125.17.7.
do.	16/5/16		Temp LIEUT W.R. LAW promoted temp. CAPTAIN under A.O.R. 12/3/15	Ref. A.Q.125/19.

T2134. Wt. W708—776. 500000. 4/15. Sir J. C. & S.

Army Form C. 2118.

WAR DIARY
or
INTELLIGENCE SUMMARY.

(Erase heading not required.)

FOLLOWER VII

Instructions regarding War Diaries and Intelligence Summaries are contained in F. S. Regs., Part II. and the Staff Manual respectively. Title pages will be prepared in manuscript.

Place	Date	Hour	Summary of Events and Information	Remarks and references to Appendices
LARK HILL	19/5/16		2/LIEUT W.F. LUCKMAN appointed temp LIEUT under A.A.C. 1572/15	RH
do	24/5/16		Temp LIEUT F. LUCKMAN appointed SIGNALLING OFFICER vice CAPT. LAW	RH
do	28/5/16		MAJOR N.H. ENGLAND was thrown from his horse and fractured his leg. MAJOR CLAUGHTON appointed acting O/C ADJUTANT which was subsequently taken over by CAPT. BROUGHTON	RH
HENHAM PARK WANGFORD	16/6/16		Battalion moved from LARKHILL TO HENHAM PARK near WANGFORD, SUFFOLK	RH
Rft r Rft 86 do	6/6/16 14/		484 Japanese Rifles & Bayonets returned to Ordnance	RH
do	29/6/16		390 Short Rifles M.L.E. taken on charge of Battalion	RB
do	3/7/16		100 Short Rifles M.L.E. taken on charge of Battalion	RB

Army Form C. 2118.

WAR DIARY
or
INTELLIGENCE SUMMARY.
(Erase heading not required.)

Instructions regarding War Diaries and Intelligence Summaries are contained in F. S. Regs., Part II. and the Staff Manual respectively. Title pages will be prepared in manuscript.

Place	Date	Hour	Summary of Events and Information	Remarks and references to Appendices
HENHAM PARK WANGFORD (Ref. 1" Sh. 88)	6/7/16		MAJOR GEN. F.W.B LANDON chief inspector of Q.M.G. services expressed himself satisfied with the appearance and turnout of the transport of the unit	W/H
do.	11/7/16		4 LEWIS GUNS taken on charge of the battalion	W/H Ref. 2 m S
do	26/7/16		62nd Division inspected by HIS MAJESTY KING GEORGE V. 186TH BRIGADE marched from HENHAM PARK to WORLINGHAM at which point His Majesty stood to take the salute. "HIS MAJESTY the KING was graciously pleased to express his high appreciation of the appearance and marching of the division, and instructed the G.O.C to convey HIS MAJESTY'S approval to all ranks."	D O dated 26/7/16
do	24/8/16		Extract from "LONDON GAZETTE" of 20TH SEPTEMBER 1916 — 2nd Lt (Temp Capt) G. BROUGHTON to be adjutant vice Capt (Temp Major) N.A. ENGLAND, 24 Aug 1916 W/H	B.O 228 21/9/16
do	23/9/16		Extract from W.O letter 121/8543(M) of 21/6/16 — 62nd (W.R) Division will Concentrate for service in France at War Establishment Part VII	
BEDFORD (Ref. 1" Sht. 147)	3/10/16		2/6 Batt. of Wellington Regt moved from HENHAM to BEDFORD	

1577 Wt.W10791/1773 500,000 1/15 D. D. & L. A.D.S.S./Forms/C. 2118.

WAR DIARY
or
INTELLIGENCE SUMMARY.
(Erase heading not required.)

Army Form C. 2118.

Place	Date	Hour	Summary of Events and Information	Remarks and references to Appendices
BEDFORD	2/1/17		Extract from Brigade orders 2/1/17 :— "The following Officers N.C.O's and men have been selected to form part of the Advance Guard Party Draft Mortar Battery of the Brigade :— 2/Lieut M.E. BORNEMAN 3154 Cpl E. CROWTHER 3146 Cpl H. GREEN 4709 Pte A. Brown, 3011 Pte L. Bentley, 3600 Pte M. Brady, 2074 Pte G. Featherstone, 3390 Pte J. Simpson, 2842 Pte R. Charlton, 3308 Pte H. Ridley, 3434 Pte R.H.B. Lemster, 2846 Pte J. Bowen (Batmen)	Brig. orders 2/1/17 dated 2/1/17 W.J.L.
BEDFORD	4/1/17		ORDER OF THE DAY issued by Maj. Gen. Braithwaite containing farewell message from His Majesty the King to 62nd Division on the eve of their departure overseas	W.J.L.
do.	4/1/17	9 a.m.	Farewell Service of Holy Communion at St. Paul's church BEDFORD before proceeding on active service.	W.J.L.
do.	14/1/17		2/6 DUKE OF WELLINGTONS REGT left BEDFORD for FRANCE. Right half Battalion left the Ballast Pit Sidings Bedford at 3:25 a.m. Left half Battalion left at 5 a.m.	

CONFIDENTIAL WAR DIARY

OF THE
2/6TH. BN. DUKE OF WELLINGTON'S WEST RIDING REGT (T.F.)

FROM JANUARY XIth 1917 TO FEBRUARY XXVIIIth 1917.

VOLUME IV

Army Form C. 2118.

WAR DIARY
or
INTELLIGENCE SUMMARY.

2/6 Duke of Wellington's Regt.

(Erase heading not required.)

Instructions regarding War Diaries and Intelligence Summaries are contained in F. S. Regs., Part II. and the Staff Manual respectively. Title pages will be prepared in manuscript.

Place	Date	Hour	Summary of Events and Information	Remarks and references to Appendices
BEDFORD	10/1/17		Orders for battalion to embark cancelled by telegram from "Eastern Command" Further orders received — Battalion to embark on January 15th 1917	WJH
do	13/1/17		A case of scarlet fever discovered in the battalion. No orders to embark for 14 days until battalion reported free from infection by A.D.M.S. BEDFORD	WJH
do	19/1/17	9.15pm	Disturbance between men of this unit and Military Police & M.P.d Guardroom took place between 9.15pm and 10pm in HIGH STREET BEDFORD	WJH
do	21/1/17		MAJOR N.A.ENGLAND returned from sick leave and reported for duty	WJH
do	3/2/17	12.45pm	Inspection of the battalion by G.O.C Northern Army (Gen. Bruce Hamilton) at Russell Park BEDFORD	WJH
do	3/2/17	5.15pm	Orders received from Eastern Command for battalion to embark on February 5th 1917	WJH
do	5/2/17	7am & 8.15am	Batt. left Ballast Pit Sidings in trains X 290 and X 291. 1st train reached SOUTHAMPTON docks at 12.30 p.m. and 2nd train at 1.35 pm.	WJH
			Batt. crossed from Southampton to HAVRE in 3 vessels — CAESAREA carrying 9 officers 376 O.R.	
			MONA'S QUEEN 13 officers 338 O.R. HUNTSCRAFT 11 officers 339 O.R. — Total 33 officers 953 O.R.	
HAVRE	5/2/17 to 6/2/17		NOMINAL ROLL of Officers landing — Lt Col Heckstall Smith, Majors N.A England, Captains N Prince, J Andrews S. Broughton (adj) E Bennett, H.K. Gaunt, A. Booth, J.M Somerset, Lieuts J.J Hagh, H.C Mackay, W.S Smith, J.B Codling, W.J Luckman, R Price, W.S Smith, J.C. Sheerman Shad, 2/Lieut...	WJH

1577 Wt. W10791/1773 500,000 1/15 D. D. & L. A.D.S.S./Forms/C. 2118.

2/6th Bn. Wellingtons Regt.

Army Form C. 2118.

WAR DIARY
or
INTELLIGENCE SUMMARY.
(Erase heading not required.)

Instructions regarding War Diaries and Intelligence Summaries are contained in F. S. Regs., Part II. and the Staff Manual respectively. Title pages will be prepared in manuscript.

Place	Date	Hour	Summary of Events and Information	Remarks and references to Appendices
LE HAVRE	6/2/17		NOMINAL ROLL OF Officers (cont) 2Lts. W.m. Harington, J. Nightingale, H. Jackson, R.M. Kimbush, Stockdale, G. Goeing, Jackman, C. Stafford, J. Howell, R. Petrie. Captain S. Handcock R.A.M.C. Rev. J. Sugd C.F. Nov. 2t (?) M. M. Dermott. Captain Kirsoff (Royal Scots attd a/c Staff), 2nd A. Somerville and 2Lt J. Broughton embarked with 188th Inf. Bde Headquarters. Total Strength of Officers — 36	W.H.
do	6/2/17	8 A.M.	Proceeded to Docks Rest Camp LE HAVRE	W.H.
do	8/2/17	12.2 A.M.	Entrained at Point 4 (Battn less 3 officers 150 O.R.)	W.H.
BELLE EGLISE LOUVENCOURT	8/2/17	7.45 A.M.	Train train reached rail-head at BELLE EGLISE and marched to rest billets at LOUVENCOURT.	W.H.
do (map. Sheets 11 G 5 & 01)	9/2/17	12.01 A.M.	Remainder of battalion reached rail-head at ACHEUX and marched to rest billets at LOUVENCOURT. Billets occupied — Nos. 9, 14, 18, 19, 39, 40, 49 A, 51, 55, 69, 67, 79, 72, 73, 79, 63, 82, 84, 95, 96, 107, 114, 116, 123, 148.	W.H.
do	13/2/17		Four Company Commanders & Intelligence Officer proceeded to Burn Hook O. 4. d to be attached to 16th Direct Rgt. in the line for instruction.	A.
do	14/2/17		Rd proceeded by Colonne gfroth to Mailly Maillet & there took over the Billets of the 1/5 Dorset Rgt.	A.
Mailly Maillet	17/2/17		R.d. relieved 2/5 Duke of Wellingtons Rgt. in Trenches, 4 1/6 Gs. BURNWORK Q. 4. d. Four Companies were disposed in front line holding Block Shell holes as POSTS, and two Companies were in	A.S.

1577 Wt. W10791/1773 500,000 1/15 D. D. & L. A.D.S.S./Forms/C. 2118.

Army Form C. 2118.

WAR DIARY
or
INTELLIGENCE SUMMARY.

(Erase heading not required.)

Instructions regarding War Diaries and Intelligence Summaries are contained in F. S. Regs., Part II. and the Staff Manual respectively. Title pages will be prepared in manuscript.

Place	Date	Hour	Summary of Events and Information	Remarks and references to Appendices
MAILLY- MAILLET	17.2.17	9.p.m.	Were in support at BURN WARK.	A.C.
BEAUMONT HAMEL	21.2.17	6.p.m.	Bn was relieved by Newfoundland and Irish Fusiliers and marched was sent to BOLTON CAMP where it remained. Whilst in the line Bn Casualties were - Two Officers & two men Killed in 3.R. Wounded... 7 O.R. 3 (O) R.R. 3 Wounded Shell Shock 1 Off 13. O.R. One Severely wounded whilst accompanying a Wiring Party	A.C.
BOLTON CAMP	25.2.17	2 p.m	A & B Coys sent to Pont 86 Admir O/C 2 nd Lieut R. Marcheson Returning to V RAVINE. 1 Peaceful Bivouac in the huts till evening.	A.C.
BLO	26.2.17	8.30 a.m.	Remainder of Bn - and H.Q proceeded to Pont 86 and rested the afternoon	A.C.
POINT...86	26.2.17	3.30 p.m.	Bn proceeded via V RAVINE to ARTILLERY LANE & then on. When R.O. and D by were quartered A & B Coys proceeded to occupy Front Area Positions BEAUREGARD ALLEY from L.33.a. to L.38.C. (C Coy was in support) In SAFETY TRENCH L.33.a.0.	A.C.
ARTILLERY LANE	27.2.17	12.30 p.m.	H.Q moved up from R.I.C Central to SAFETY TRENCH L.33.a. While 7.9.15 Coys advanced and occupied ORCHARD ALLEY L.21.a.r.d.' Coy Bivouc'd in Strong position QUARRY TRENCH L.21.C. O Coy moved from SAFETY TRENCH to BEAUREGARD DUGOUTS L.32.C A Coy continued 1 Patrol from ORCHARD ALLEY and SUNKEN ROAD L.15.C.d.	A.C.
SAFETY TRENCH	1.3.17	6 a.m.	Bn were relieved by 2 nd Grenadiers. All our 1st & Reserved moved to HAWTHORN RIDGE. G.10.6.	A.C.

86/62

Vol 3

2.V.
4 sheets

Confidential

War Diary

of the

2/6th Bn. Duke of Wellington's West Riding Regt. (T.F.).

From. March 1st 1917
To.   March 31st 1917

S.W. Short Lt. Col.
Comdg. 2/6 Duke of Wellington' Regt.

Original

Original

Army Form C. 2118.

WAR DIARY

of

26th Duke of Wellington's Regt

INTELLIGENCE SUMMARY.

(Erase heading not required.)

Instructions regarding War Diaries and Intelligence Summaries are contained in F. S. Regs., Part II. and the Staff Manual respectively. Title pages will be prepared in manuscript.

Place	Date	Hour	Summary of Events and Information	Remarks and references to Appendices
HAWTHORN RIDGE	3/3/17	10 a.m.	The following Officers reported to Bn. HdQrs. from HQrs. 5th Army for duty with the Bn. 2/Lt. K. Ackroyd. 2/Lt. A.H. Scott. 2/Lt. C. Scott. 2/Lt. L. Crabtree.	A
do	3/3/17		Bn. Casualties whilst in trenches from 26/2/17 to 3/3/17. Killed in trenches SUNKEN ROAD or L.I.S.c.td. incl:- Killed and Died of wounds (O): i.e. 2910 Pte Duxbury A. 2977 Pte Clive S. Branch " Pipkin J. 3009 " Earley G. 8872 " Rowe S. 2809 " Auckland C.	A
			Wounded — 13	
do	3/3/17	2 p.m.	Bn. proceeded into billets at ENGLEBELMER, escorted by bugling band.	A
ENGLE-BELMER	9/3/17	1 p.m.	"C" Company left ENGLEBELMER and proceeded into billets at LEALVILLERS for a period of 10 days providing working parties to R.E. the billing duty next 3 days in trenches 3 nights as a reinforcement I.B.C. ("C" Company) (Apr. Lewr.)	A
do	10/3/17	10 a.m.	100 men of "B" Company proceeded to AVELUY WOOD under O.R.P. Sergeant for purposes of facing, hurdling and wood cutting. Their accommodation was to be billets.	A
do	11/3/17	8 a.m.	110 O.Rs of "A" Company under 2/Lt. (blk) proceeded to HAMEL & returned on Engines Accommodated in Dug-outs in BEAUMONT HAMEL or HAWTHORN RIDGE and Bn. A.S.S. Lorries. Daily carried out these movements with Tour Light F Regiment Tunnel.	A
do	12/3/17	8 a.m.	The following draft reported for duty from (blk) base taken on the strength of the Bn. 1 Officer (2/Lt. C. H. Cooper) and 144 O.R.	A

Army Form C. 2118.

WAR DIARY
or
INTELLIGENCE SUMMARY.
(Erase heading not required.)

Place	Date	Hour	Summary of Events and Information	Remarks and references to Appendices
ENGLEBE- LMER.	15/3/17	1 p.m.	The Bn. moved from ENGLEBELMER to BOIS D'HYLAND and R.8. Central, preceded by the Billeting Party, and received Dug-outs & Shelters in this area, arriving about 4.30 p.m. About 7.30 p.m. the two Coys. detailed to trace the Accommodation and proceed forward to MIRAUMONT, (these Bn. H.Q. and 'D' Company occupied Dug-outs Cellars & Shelters in & near R.4.c.5.9. 'C' Coy. were Accommodated in HINDENBURG TRENCH (R.3.b.3.8.); 'B' Coy in the BRICKFIELDS (L.29.c+d.) and of the MIRAUMONT-BEAUREGARD DOVECOTE road at L.34.b.3.8. 'A' Coy. remained at the Brick Quarries R.10.4.9. "20 ft DEEP" (R.4.a.2.1.). The Bn. was ordered to MIRAUMONT to act as Support Bn. to 186th Inf. Bde. attack on ACHIET-LE-PETIT.	K.S.
MIRAUMONT	18/3/17	2.45 p.m.	Bn. had orders to proceed to ACHIET-LE-PETIT and parades at 2.45 p.m. This order was cancelled as soon as the Bn. was in the road, and the Bn. returned to its old Quarters in MIRAUMONT. (N.B. The Bn. had attacked as Advance Guard to the force forming the Strong).	K.S.
do	19/3/17 to 24/3/17	8.0 a.m.	The Bn. was employed on the MIRAUMONT – ACHIET-LE-PETIT road, making two foot bridges for the passage of Artillery & transport, helping the Engineers to build bridges &c. This work was of the utmost importance until completed the withdrawal of Enemy to CAMBRAI line could not be adequately followed up.	K.S.
do	25/3/17	8.45 a.m.	Advance Billeting Party (consisting of 1 Officer and 20 O.Rs. proceeded to the neighbourhood of LOGEAST WOOD (G.1.a.0.1.) for the purpose of finding accommodation for the Bn.	K.S.
do	26/3/17		Bn. left MIRAUMONT and proceeded to LOGEAST WOOD for the purpose of occupying Dug-outs & Shelters. During the day hour on the roads and railway at PUISIEUX two contained.	K.S.
LOGEAST WOOD	27/3/17		Bn. still employed on roads &c. in PUISIEUX, with exception of a few over left behind for Erection and Completion of Shelters.	K.S.

1577 Wt.W10791/1773 500,000 1/15 D. D. & L. A.D.S.S./Forms/C. 2118.

Army Form C. 2118.

WAR DIARY
or
INTELLIGENCE SUMMARY.
(Erase heading not required.)

Instructions regarding War Diaries and Intelligence Summaries are contained in F. S. Regs., Part II. and the Staff Manual respectively. Title pages will be prepared in manuscript.

Place	Date	Hour	Summary of Events and Information	Remarks and references to Appendices
ENGLEBELMER	12/3/17	10.0 a.m.	Lt (A/C) J. MacKillop (sick) Embarked for ENGLAND.	
MIRAUMONT	17/3/17		Major C/M Ford (8th Suffolk R.A.) departed for duty, & took over command of the Bn.	
do	22/3/17	2 p.m.	2/Lt E. Clapham reported for duty, & was taken on the strength of the Bn.	
ENGLEBELMER	4/3/17		Lt R.S. Sexton (wounded) left for ENGLAND, & was struck off the strength of the Bn.	
LOBEAST WOOD	27/3/17	4 p.m.	A draft of 24 men from Reserve Bn reported, & were taken on the war strength.	
do	30/3/17	10 a.m.	The following Officers reported for duty, & were taken on the strength:- (From Res. Bn.) 2/Lt C.H. Clegg (posted to "B" Coy.) 2/Lt C.G. Carr (" " "A" ").	

ORIGINAL.

"CONFIDENTIAL."

WAR DIARY.

OF

2/6 Bn Duke of Wellington's Regt.

FROM 1-4-1917.   TO. 30-4-1917.

VOLUME No. 4.

Vol 4

S.V.
4 sheets.

2/6 Duke of Wellington's Regt

ORIGINAL

Army Form C. 2118.

WAR DIARY
or
INTELLIGENCE SUMMARY.

(Erase heading not required.)

Instructions regarding War Diaries and Intelligence Summaries are contained in F. S. Regs., Part II. and the Staff Manual respectively. Title pages will be prepared in manuscript.

Place	Date	Hour	Summary of Events and Information	Remarks and references to Appendices
LOGEAST WOOD	1.4.17	2.8.p	Coy. Sgt. Major Clarke ('A' Coy) mentioned in list of statistics in hands of War Office service while training troops in ENGLAND.	A.1
do	3.4.17	8.0 a.m	Advance Party of 4 Officers and 50 Other Ranks to GOMMECOURT for the purpose of preparing & improving accommodation for the Bn in the village.	A.1
do	4.4.17	5 pm	Bn. moved into GOMMECOURT area in Divisional Reserve, the 62nd Div. relieving from the line from the 7th Div. on the night of April 4th/5th.	A.1
GOMMECOURT	5.4.17		Bn. on working parties and training.	A.1
do	6.4.17		The Commander of the VII Corps, under authority delegated to him, has awarded the Military Medal to the undermentioned Other Ranks of this Bn. ("Divisional Routine Orders" by Major-General W.P. Braithwaite, C.B.) :— 5107 Pte J.T. Mussey ⅔ West Riding Regiment. "Whilst in BUDGEON TRENCH on the 1st March 1917 at 11.45 a.m. a shell burst in front of pais, killing two men & wounding several others. Despite heavy shell fire Pte Mussey, in company with Pte J. Williams went out & attended to the wounded, showing great courage & devotion to duty. Later Pte Mussey again under heavy shell fire went out & attended to his wounded men, who had been wounded whilst proceeding to Bn H.Q." (V. Corps MM.257, dated 2/4/17). 4564 Pte J. Williams 2/6 West Riding Rgt. "Whilst in GUDGEON TRENCH on the 1st March 1917, at 11.45 a.m., a shell burst in front of pais, Exploding L.G. ammunition, killing two men and wounding several others. In spite of heavy shell fire Pte Williams in company with Pte Mussey went out & attended the wounded, showing utter disregard for his own safety and strong devotion to duty." (V. Corps MM.257, dated 2/4/17).	A.1

ORIGINAL

Army Form C. 2118.

Instructions regarding War Diaries and Intelligence
Summaries are contained in F. S. Regs., Part II.
and the Staff Manual respectively. Title pages
will be prepared in manuscript.

WAR DIARY
or
INTELLIGENCE SUMMARY.
(Erase heading not required.)

Place	Date	Hour	Summary of Events and Information	Remarks and references to Appendices
GOMMIECOURT	10.4.17	5 a.m.	Bn moved up to a point East of MORY on the MORY ECOUST Road, and owing to the breaking of the HINDENBURG LINE further South, and the apparent absence of Enemy in BULLECOURT, it had been thought possible that two pieces had been located by the Enemy. Owing however to the absence of the Tanks which should have supported the Australians attacking on our right, no attack was made. The Bn returned to billets in GOMMIECOURT about 11 a.m.	A.1.
do	11.4.17 4 a.m.		The Bn again moved up to three point East of MORY in support of the expected advance of the 185th Bde at BULLECOURT, who were sending patrols into patrols on the left of the Anzac attack. As however the attack was unsuccessful, the Bn again returned to GOMMIECOURT.	A.2
do	12.4.17 5 p.m.		Preceded by a large party for the improvement of Military Sanitation accommodation, the Bn moved up into MORY and took over billets vacated by the 1/7th Manchester Regt. The 186th Bde relieved the 185th Bde in the line on the night of Apr. 12/13, two Bns being in reserve, just prior to relief it was thought the Enemy had vacated BULLECOURT, 1185th Bde sent out fighting patrols to verify this, 1865 Bde holding themselves in readiness to push forward if an event was BULLECOURT was still in the hands of the Enemy, the relief being completed.	A.3
MORY	13.4.17 10 p.m.		2/Lt Dinsdale and 18 men on the night of April 13-14 went out to Dummy trench & West of BULLECOURT with Bangalore Torpedoes. Three of these were laid in the wire under machine gun and rifle fire from Sucrerie. The party returned to the British lines with the slight casualty of one successful accomplishment of this operation has been due to the courage, discipline and efficiency of all those engaged. (Extract from Bde Orders No. 58 of 21.4.17.) "The Army Commander wishes his appreciation of the B. of three platoons, 2/5th N.F. conveyed to the Officers of the N.C.O.'s and men who carried out the demolitions by BANGALORE Torpedoes on the night 13/14 April. It is hoped to carry to them in person to-morrow."	A.5

ORIGINAL.

Army Form C. 2118.

WAR DIARY
or
INTELLIGENCE SUMMARY.
(Erase heading not required.)

Instructions regarding War Diaries and Intelligence Summaries are contained in F. S. Regs., Part II. and the Staff Manual respectively. Title pages will be prepared in manuscript.

Place	Date	Hour	Summary of Events and Information	Remarks and references to Appendices
LOGEAST WOOD	1.4.17		Major McLaughlin reported for duty. No Scout in command.	A.S.
MORY	18.4.17	10.30 a.m.	While in Camp in the MORY BLOUST road, "A" and "D" (less F.E.C. Family) parties hit by shells. Capt. N.C. Prince was killed. And Capt Rhodes/Kenk D.D.E. Hugh. Pearse wounded. O.R.'s as under Killed : 4916 Pte Rivers A. 6127 Pte Allsopp J.H. 3600 Pte Beard H. 3115 Pte Wright R. Acting Sergt. Wounded : 13 O.Rs.	A.S.
LOGEAST WOOD	7.4.17		4785 Qur. Ashbury H. died in hospital.	A.S.
MORY	18.4.17		"A" & "D" Coys. support Band Camp to K & R.E. S/E of MORY, where for the following days they kept them full by the O.C.'s. The 'B' & 'C' Coys.	A.S.
do	19.4.17			A.S.
do	20.4.17		Injured when on a Working-Party in EGOUST — 1 O.Rs.	A.S.
do	15.4.17 } 17.4.17 }		Wounded while on Working Parties I.C. 5 O.Rs.	A.S.
do	21.4.17	7.30 p.m.	2/Lt. M. Hardaker reported for duty. And was taken to the Camp at YTRES, R.E. (Stores of Rear B2)	R.S.
do	22.4.17		52.01 Pte. Wall W. On a scout by a bombing accident. Sent forward to hospital.	B.S.
do	27.4.17		2/Lt. J.L. Arrowpool (London Regt.) reported for duty. And was taken to the strength of the B.C. Reinforcements - 3 O.Rs.	A.S.
do	27.4.17		Corp. Sgt. Suj. Shoemaker returned from Hospital for duty with "D" Coy	A.S.
do	28.4.17	3 a.m.	2909 Sgt A. Smith while in charge of a Guard on a R.E. dump in EGOUST was slightly Wounded in the head with shrapnel.	A.S.
do	26.4.17		267111 Pte J.W. Bancroft died in hospital of wounds received on Apr 18th.	A.S.

A.8534 Wt. W4973/M687 750,000 8/16 D. D. & L. Ltd. Forms/C.2118/13.

CONFIDENTIAL.

WAR DIARY

OF

2/6TH. BN. DUKE OF WELLINGTON'S REGT.

FROM MAY 1ST 1917 TO MAY 31ST 1917

VOLUME 4.

Army Form C. 2118.

WAR DIARY
or
INTELLIGENCE SUMMARY.
(Erase heading not required.)

2/6 Duke of Wellingtons Regt

Instructions regarding War Diaries and Intelligence Summaries are contained in F.S. Regs., Part II. and the Staff Manual respectively. Title pages will be prepared in manuscript.

Place	Date	Hour	Summary of Events and Information	Remarks and references to Appendices
MORY	1/5/17		Battalion in Camp at B.28.a Central (FRANCE Sheet 57c N.W)	Ints
do	do	9 pm	C & D Coys under Major CLAUGHTON relieved the 22nd MANCHESTER REGT & took over the line W of BULLECOURT (FRANCE Sheet 51.B.S.W.4) from U.27.a.6.7 to U.20.d.9.4. Batt HQrs at U.26.C.7.0. The line was held by means of posts with the main body behind the Railway Embankment at U.26.C.7.0.	do
MORY	2/5/17	9pm	HQs, A & B Coys under Lt Col S M FORD proceeded to the Railway Embankment at U.26.C.7.0 in order to take part in an attack which the 62nd Division was making at 3.40 am on the 3rd MAY 1917 on BULLECOURT (FRANCE SHEET 51.B.S.W.4) & trenches of the HINDENBURG LINE West of BULLECOURT. Orders of the Batt Commander (Lt Col S M FORD) attached herewith.	Appendices 1 + 2
RAILWAY EMBANKMENT U.26.C.7.0.	3/5/17		The Battalion suffered severe losses during the attack on two stations. Casualties. Officers. 1 Killed (LIEUT R O'NEILL), 5 Wounded (CAPT. S J RHODES, CAPT. J M SOMERVELL, CAPT. C D BENNETT, 2/LT W G KINGHORN, R M WIMBUSH) 3 Missing (CAPT W K LAW, 2/LT W STOCKDALE, & C HOLROYD), Other Ranks Killed 15 Wounded 155 Missing 88	Ints

Army Form C. 2118.

WAR DIARY
or
INTELLIGENCE SUMMARY.
(Erase heading not required.)

1/6 Duke of Wellington's Regt

Place	Date	Hour	Summary of Events and Information	Remarks and references to Appendices
RAILWAY EMBANKMENT U26.c.7.0	3/5/17	10pm	The Battalion proceeded to Camp at MORY, B.28.a. Central (FRANCE Sheet 57c N.W.) being relieved by the 2/5th DUKE of WELLINGTONS REGT to whom 2 Officers + 80 ORs were lent.	1/15
MORY B.28.a Central	4/5/17	9pm	The Camp of this Batt" was taken over by the 2nd Batt" GORDON HIGHLANDERS + the Batt" proceeded to the RAILWAY EMBANKMENT at U.26.c.7.0 (FRANCE 51B SW 4) to take over the line from U.26.c.7.0. to U.26.d.5.0. from the 2/5th DUKE of WELLINGTONS. Posts were established on a line U.27.a.5.3. to U.26.b.8.7.	2/15
RAILWAY EMBANKMENT U.26.c.7.0	5/5/17	2am	2/Lt T.S. SHACKLETON was killed on the Embankment by a shell.	3/15
do	6/5/17	10pm	The Battalion was relieved at night by the 2/4th Duke of Wellingtons Regt + proceeded to Camp near MORY (B.15.d.2.5.)	4/15
MORY (B.15.d.2.5.)	7/5/17		Battalion was placed under the orders of G.O.C. 185th Inf. Bde to whom they were acting as support. Training was carried out daily.	5/15

Army Form C. 2118.

WAR DIARY
or
INTELLIGENCE SUMMARY.
(Erase heading not required.)

Instructions regarding War Diaries and Intelligence Summaries are contained in F. S. Regs., Part II. and the Staff Manual respectively. Title pages will be prepared in manuscript.

2/6 Duke of Wellington Rgt

Place	Date	Hour	Summary of Events and Information	Remarks and references to Appendices
MORY	10/5/17		On the night of the 10th, 11th & 12th inst the Battalion was ordered to harrass the L'HOMME MORT (B17 a 9.9 sheet 57 C NW) arriving there at 9 pm & returning to Camp at B 15 d 2.5 at daybreak.	1/t
do	12/5/17		Operations. Meritorious Service during. The G.O.C. wishes to place on record his high appreciation of the gallant conduct of the following NCOs men whose names been brought to his notice by Brigade Reserves & Commanding Officers. 265033 Sgt J.M. WALKER. 266023 C/k G. MASON. 300077 P't STANDISH. A. 300078 P't SCHOFIELD. W. 127709 P't MELLING. J.W. 13365 P't SIMPSON. W. 266680 P't BROUGHTON. N. 300061 P't GRUNWELL. H. 300067 P't HEDGES. G. 266901 P't PICKUP. W. 109441 P't QUINN. H. 266685 P't ALTON. A.E. 266683 P't EDMONDSON. H. 266806 P't HARWOOD. J.T. 3/9738 P't MANN J. 266740 P't YOUNG. H. The above party exploded bangalore torpedoes under enemy wire on night of 14/15 Apr 1917	1/t
do	13/5/17		Owing to recent heavy casualties the 2/6th & 2/6th DUKE of WELLINGTON'S REGIMENTS were formed into a Composite Battalion for the purpose of taking over the line.	

Army Form C. 2118.

WAR DIARY or INTELLIGENCE SUMMARY.

(Erase heading not required.)

1/6 Duke of Wellingtons Regt

Place	Date	Hour	Summary of Events and Information	Remarks and references to Appendices
MORY (B.15.d.25.)	13/5/17		14 Officers & 251 O.Rs being formed into 2 Companies & attached to the 2/4th DUKE of WELLINGTONS REGT under Lt.COL. H.E.P.NASH, the H/q of the 2/4th DUKE of WELLINGTONS proceeding to the transport lines at ERVILLERS (B.13.a.8.7 Sheet 57c N.W.). Two Composite batt's held the line of the Railway Embankment at U.25.d.7.1. to the Road junction at T.24.a.8.5, having a series of posts on a line from U.20.d.3.3 to U.13.c.7.3, until relieved by the 2/5th K.O.Y.L.I. on the night of the 20th MAY 1917. Casualties of men of this Batt" during the period 8 O.Rs 1 Killed 8 wounded.	MAP R/3 51/5 WH 5/5 WH 6/15
ERVILLERS 20/5/17 (B.13.a.2.5. Sheet 57c N.W.)			Batt" moved into billets at COURCELLES (A.15.d.) where the battalion carried out training duties up to the 29th MAY 1917	6/15
to COURCELLES (A.15.d. Sheet 57c N.W.)	21/5/17		Operations. Meritorious Service during. The G.O.C. wishes to place on record his high appreciation of the gallant conduct of the following men which have been brought to his notice by Brigadier Generals + O/c formations - 267114 Pte DOBSON T.A. 266445 Pte JOHNSON R.S. 265385 Pte GARRETT J. 267220 Pte FISHER J. 266285 C/µ GOLDING G.A. 266356 Pte STEVENS R. 266606 Pte HARWOOD J.T. 266940 Pte ROBINSON A. for operation on May 3rd 19.17.	D.O.537 2/5/17 6/15

Army Form C. 2118.

WAR DIARY
or
INTELLIGENCE SUMMARY.
(Erase heading not required.)

Place	Date	Hour	Summary of Events and Information	Remarks and references to Appendices
ERVILLERS B+ F 60+ 5 COURCELLES A15d. Sheet 57c N.W.	28/5/17		Honours & Rewards. The Commander of the 5th Corps under authority delegated to him has awarded MILITARY MEDALS to the undermentioned NCOs & men for gallantry during the operations which commenced on May 3rd 1917. 266876 L/Cpl HODKINSON. A 267064 Pte BATES. J 266338 Pte BIRKETT J 266771 Pte MILLS. A.E.	
do	29/5/17		The following Officers joined the Bn as reinforcements - 2/Lts E WOOD, A G PARKINSON, A BRAY, E. RAIREY, E. DUNVILLE, E SCOTT.	
do	29/5/17	11am	Batt proceeded to Hts Camp at BRADFORD CAMP, ACHIET-LE-PETIT (Guarago Sheet 57c N.W.) there training has continued 2/Lt S.B MANN joined the batt as a reinforcement	

Army Form C. 2118.

6th Duke of Wellington's Regt

WAR DIARY
or
INTELLIGENCE SUMMARY.
(Erase heading not required.)

Place	Date	Hour	Summary of Events and Information	Remarks and references to Appendices
ACHIET-LE-PETIT (G.1.a.9.0. Sheet 57cNW)	29/5/17		Under authority granted by His Majesty the King, the Field Marshal Commanding in Chief has awarded the following decorations for gallant meritorious service during the attack on May 3rd 1917 – MILITARY CROSS. LIEUT. W.F LUCKMAN. This officer was in charge of 2 signalling parties who were laying wire from the Railway Embankment, ECOUST to the Sunken Road in the HINDENBURG LINE W of BULLECOURT during the attack May 3rd. His own party became casualties. He went out to find the other party which had met the same fate. For a long time he endeavoured to establish telephone communication under very heavy shell fire. Finding it impossible he took charge of a party of stragglers establishing in the Sunken Rd where he remained all day, helping to bring in the wounded at night. On the 4th May he went out to sight advanced posts. One of the posts was blown up. 2/0 of the garrison was killed & the remainder wounded. LIEUT. LUCKMAN continued arranging the position & he just thought was in a place under cover fire a very heavy bombardment. This officer showed great gallantry, resource & initiative under heavy fire from little dugouts for his own safety. His example has been an	DO 571 29/5/17 Ans

Army Form C. 2118.

WAR DIARY
or
INTELLIGENCE SUMMARY.
(Erase heading not required.)

Place	Date	Hour	Summary of Events and Information	Remarks and references to Appendices
ACHIET-LE-PETIT	29/5/17		MILITARY CROSS. 6872 Company Sgt-Major Charles H. GARTSIDE. — "Showed conspicuous gallantry & devotion to duty during the attack of the 3rd May. He organised a party & held the first German trench in the HINDENBURG LINE N. of BULLECOURT & collected another party & attacked the second hostile trench. He was unable to reach it as most of his party were casualties. He returned, organised another party & through devotion of the first during trench held positions in the line till such time as he was ordered to withdraw. His disregard of personal safety & fine example against uncoomon this moment him this name his gallantly mentioned to me by MAJOR COCKBURN, WEST RIDING REGT. & was given to me testimony of my own Officers." Distinguished Conduct Medal 265530 Company Sgt-Major J. MAUDE.— "Showed conspicuous gallantry & devotion to duty during the attack of 3rd May 1917. This N.C.O. showed fine qualities of leadership & was a good example of courage, coolness under heavy shell & machine gun fire. He rallied & organised parties who had lost direction & restored the morale of the men."	A.D.5.7.1 24/5/17 6/6

A5834 Wt.W4973/M687 750,000 8/16 D.D.&L. Ltd. Form/C.2118/13.

Army Form C. 2118.

WAR DIARY
or
INTELLIGENCE SUMMARY.
(Erase heading not required.)

Instructions regarding War Diaries and Intelligence Summaries are contained in F.S. Regs., Part II. and the Staff Manual respectively. Title pages will be prepared in manuscript.

5/6 Duke of Wellington Regt

Place	Date	Hour	Summary of Events and Information	Remarks and references to Appendices
ACHIET-LE-PETIT	29/5/17		In the HINDENBURG LINE, N of BULLECOURT. The enemy two enemy machine guns enfiladed, barraged the trenches holding up the advance. After strong bombing attacks the look up a position in which were in the enemy's line thrust out during the day only were driven out at night.	£/15 DO 57/ 29/5/17
			Distinguished Conduct Medal 265926 Sgt J.T. McLEOD. "Showed conspicuous gallantry, devotion to duty during the attack of the 3rd May. This N.C.O. in charge of a machine gun section worked through the first hostile trench W of BULLECOURT his gun was knocked out. He reorganized another party, pushed forward. When they had all become casualties he returned collected another party of bombers began attacked the trench. This party met the same fate. Sgt McLEOD remained in the enemy lines using his gun till those refused to retire. Throughout the whole day he showed great courage, gave valuable assistance in reforming the now disorganised great qualities of leadership."	£/15 DO 57/ 29/5/17

S.W. POSEY Lt Col
Comdg 5/6 Duke of Wellington Regt

CONFIDENTIAL

WAR DIARY.

OF.

2/6TH BN. DUKE OF WELLINGTON'S REGT.

FROM JUNE 1ST 1917.   TO JUNE 30TH 1917.

VOLUME 5.

Army Form C.2118.

WAR DIARY
or
INTELLIGENCE SUMMARY.

(Erase heading not required.)

1/6 Duke of Wellington Rgt

Instructions regarding War Diaries and Intelligence Summaries are contained in F. S. Regs., Part II. and the Staff Manual respectively. Title pages will be prepared in manuscript.

Place	Date	Hour	Summary of Events and Information	Remarks and references to Appendices
ACHIET-LE-PETIT G.14.a.9.0.	1/6/17		Battalion carried out training daily whilst in Rest Camp.	1/6
do	10/6/17	6pm	A composite 2 companies (7 Officers + 226 ORs) under MAJOR N.A. ENGLAND took over the defence of the 62nd Division portion of the Vth CORPS 2nd Line from B.24.d.6.7. to L'HOMME MORT (inclusive) Ref.e FRANCE Sheet 57c NW with HQ at B.17.b.2.6. The remainder of the Battalion remained in Camp at ACHIET-LE-PETIT + carried out training	Appendix 1 1/6
do	13/6/17		MAJOR W. CLAUGHTON left the Batt to report to O.C. Chinese Labour Corps Base Depot, NOYELLES-SUR-MER (Authority A.G. GHQ. A/25981 of 8/6/17)	1/6
do	14/6/17		33 ORs joined the Battn as reinforcements from the 34th Infantry Base Depot.	6/6
do	17/6/17	9pm	The 2 Composite Companies under MAJOR N.A. ENGLAND have relieved in the 2nd line of defence by the 2/4th DUKE OF WELLINGTON'S REGT + returned to Camp at ACHIET-LE-PETIT, where training was continued. For defence scheme see Appendix 1.	1/6

T2134. Wt. W708-776. 500000. 4/15. Sir J.C. & S.

Army Form C. 2118.

WAR DIARY
or
INTELLIGENCE SUMMARY.
(Erase heading not required.)

Instructions regarding War Diaries and Intelligence Summaries are contained in F. S. Regs., Part II. and the Staff Manual respectively. Title pages will be prepared in manuscript.

Place	Date	Hour	Summary of Events and Information	Remarks and references to Appendices
ACHIET-LE-PETIT L.14.a.9.0 (Sheet ACHIET 57 A NE)	22/6/17		2/Lt. J. STOCKS & H.A. WALKER & 10 O.Rs joined the Battalion as reinforcement from the 34th Inf. Base Depot. ETAPLES	1/b
do	26/6/17	3.15pm	Battalion left ACHIET-LE-PETIT & marched to FAVREUIL (Sheet 57c N.W.) where they encamped at B Camp H10 a 5.6	See App 2 1/b
FAVREUIL 27/6/17 (H10 a 5.6 B. Camp) (57c NW)	27/6/17	8pm	C & D Coys were attached under the orders of O.C. 2/7th DUKE of WELLINGTONS REGT & proceeded to take over the line N.E. of NOREUIL.	1/b See App. 2
		9pm	HQrs, A & B Coys proceeded to NOREUIL (Sheet 57c NW 1/20000). HQrs of the Battalion were established at C16 a 4 8	
			A & B Coys relieved one Company of the 7th K.O.Y.L.I. (20th Division) from C10 b 4 4 to C11 c 5 5 (Sheet 57c NW) in the support line	1/b See App 3
NOREUIL (Sheet 57c NW)	29/6/17		C & D Coys held the portion of front line from U29 d 6.9 (Sheet 03.1 D.24 1/20000) to C5 d 6.5 under the orders of O.C. 2/7th DUKE of WELLINGTONS REGT Casualties O.Rs. 1 Killed 1 wounded	1/b

Army Form C. 2118.

WAR DIARY
or
INTELLIGENCE SUMMARY.
(Erase heading not required.)

1/5 Duke of Wellingtons Rgt

Place	Date	Hour	Summary of Events and Information	Remarks and references to Appendices
NOREUIL (Sheet 57°NW)	29/6/17		C & D Coys Continued to hold the front of the line allotted to them. A & B Coys in Support provided Carrying & Working Parties. Casualties 1 O.R. wounded	6/15
do	30/6/17		do. Casualties Nil.	6/15

Howard Whylaws Major
Comdg 1/5 Duke of Wellington Rgt.

"SECRET"

WAR DIARY

OF

2/6TH BN DUKE OF WELLINGTON'S REGT.

VOLUME 6.

FROM JULY 1ST 1917   TO JULY 31ST 1917

Army Form C. 2118.

WAR DIARY
or
INTELLIGENCE SUMMARY.
(Erase heading not required.)

1/6 Duke of Wellington Regt

Instructions regarding War Diaries and Intelligence Summaries are contained in F.S. Regs., Part II. and the Staff Manual respectively. Title pages will be prepared in manuscript.

Place	Date	Hour	Summary of Events and Information	Remarks and references to Appendices
NOREUIL (Sheet 57c NW) 1/20000	1/7/17	11 pm	A & B Coys relieved C & D Coys in the line from U29 d 6.9 to C5 d 8.5 (Sheet O31 - D24 1/20000) coming under the orders of O6 2/7th DUKE OF WELLINGTONS REGT. C & D Coys occupying from C10 d 4.4 to C11 c 5.5 (Sheet 57c NW) H.Qs remained at C16 a 4.8 (Sheet 57c NW)	1/6
do	1/7/17		The following extract from list No 141 of Appointments etc appeared by the Field Marshal Commanding in Chief, the British Armies in France:- To be acting Captains whilst Commanding Companies 2 Lt (Temp Lt) C.G.C. KILNER, 2nd Lt (Temp Lt) A. SOMERVELL, 2/Lt (Temp Lt) F.E.C. SHEARME, 18th May 1917. 2nd Lt W.G. KINGHORN, 3rd May 1917 on which date he relinquished that rank wounded.	Authority A/7483/3 (62nd Div) 1/6
do	2/7/17	10:30 pm	C & D Coys formed part of a detachment under O.C. 457th FIELD COY R.E. to dig a new front line trench from U29 d 7.6 (Sheet 57c NE) to C5 d 8.6 (Sheet 57c NW). Which was accomplished before daybreak. This party was complimented on the excellence of their work.	1/6
do	3rd 7/17		Ordinary trench routine carried out.	1/6

Army Form C. 2118.

WAR DIARY
or
INTELLIGENCE SUMMARY.
(Erase heading not required.)

1/6 Duke of Wellington Rgt

Place	Date	Hour	Summary of Events and Information	Remarks and references to Appendices
NOREUIL. (SHEET 57°C NW) (20000)	5/7/17	2 am.	The Bⁿ was relieved in the NOREUIL sector by the 2/5ᵗʰ KOYLI Rgt. The relief being successfully completed by 2am. 5/7/17. The Bⁿ proceeded under canvas at FAVREUIL (H10 a.5-6) where training was carried on. Total casualties whilst holding the line were 2 killed and 6 wounded. The following reinforcements were received whilst in the line - 2 officers, 39 OR.	
FAVREUIL. (SHEET 57°C NW) 13/7/17 (20000)	13/7/17		After a weeks' training the Bⁿ proceeded to relieve the 2/5ᵗʰ West York Regt in the anglès of the LAGNICOURT sector. The Bⁿ left camp at 8-45pm 13/7/17 and proceeded to LAGNICOURT via VAULX - VRAUCOURT.	

Army Form C. 2118.

WAR DIARY
or
INTELLIGENCE SUMMARY.
(Erase heading not required.)

2/6 Duke of Wellington Regt

Place	Date	Hour	Summary of Events and Information	Remarks and references to Appendices
LAGNICOURT SHEET 57C.N.W. 1/20000	14/7/17	1.15 p.m.	The relief of the 2/6 Bn. West Yorks Regt was carried out by the 1/5th in the Left Subsector of the LAGNICOURT Sector. The line extending from C.12.a.1.0 to a point on the LAGNICOURT - QUÉANT ROAD at C.12.c.53. C.3.D. Coys occupying the forward posts and A & B Coys the support line. "B" Headquarters were at C.23.b.6.8. The relief was successfully completed by 1.15 a.m. without a single casualty. The day was quiet and ordinary Trench Routine work was carried out.	S66
—do—	17/7/17		Every thing very quiet - several Trench mortar bombs carried out - Trenches widened and deepened - duckboards put down in the support line. Engineers are also constructing dugouts around B.24.2 and in the support line. The area around B.24.4 receives a great deal of attention by the Boche artillery owing to proximity of guns - here our first casualties occurred, two men being wounded on the night 16/17 July by splinters from a shell. Capt Bennett O.D. who was commanding "B" Company was fatally wounded by a sniper whilst leaving "D" Coy Headquarters where he had been to arrange a relief.	S56
—do—	19/7/17		A & B Coys relieved the two forward Companies R & D in the front line - C & D Companies taking up the support line. The relief was successfully completed by 12 midnight 17/18 July. Patrols were sent out that had little to report.	S66
—do—	21/7/17		Very quiet up to this time - several Trench Mortars & Stokes carried out. Trenches widened - dugouts and revetted. Dugouts made in M.L.R. The Boche blew in our places to the right of the 21/22nd July. The 1/5th Bn. was relieved in the Left Subsector of the LAGNICOURT sector by the 2/6 Bn Duke of Wellington Regt. The relief was successfully completed by 12.15 a.m. 22/7/17. 1/5 Bn. Duke of Wellington to take up the support line previously occupied by the 2/6th Duke of Wellington. The B & D and "A & C" coys took up position at C.29.a.3.8. and "B & D" coys along the LAGNICOURT - ORIELLE ROAD from C.28.b.4.9. to C.17.d.6.2.	S66

Army Form C. 2118.

WAR DIARY
or
INTELLIGENCE SUMMARY.
(Erase heading not required.)

1/6 Duke of Wellington W.

Place	Date	Hour	Summary of Events and Information	Remarks and references to Appendices
VAULX-VRAUCOURT (SHEET 57 NW 1/20000)	28/7/17		After a very quiet period in outpost the 2/6 Bn Duke of Wellingtons Regt was relieved by the 2/5-Bn Duke of Wellingtons Regt on the night 24/25th July. The relief being completed by 1.30am 25/7/17. The 2/6 Bn Duke of Wellingtons proceeded to billets in VAULX-VRAUCOURT and billets occupied by the 2/5-Bn Duke of Wellingtons Regt. "C" Coy occupied the 2nd Line of Defence running from the N of MORCHIES to about C13 c 40.30.	
VAULX-VRAUCOURT (SHEET 57 NW 1/20000)	31/7/17		The 2/6 Bn Duke of Wellingtons Regt was relieved by the 2/4th Y&L Regt — the relief being completed by 12 midnight 29/30th July. The Bn proceeded to Bivouacs at FAVREUIL for Training.	

S.W. ??? Lt. Col
Comdg 2/6 Duke of Wellingtons Regt
Aug 1st 1917

Original

"SECRET"

WAR DIARY

OF

2/6TH BN DUKE OF WELLINGTON'S REGT

VOLUME 7

FROM AUG 1ST 1917

TO AUG 31ST 1917

Army Form C. 2118.

2/Bn Duke of Wellington

WAR DIARY
~~INTELLIGENCE SUMMARY~~
(Erase heading not required.)

Instructions regarding War Diaries and Intelligence Summaries are contained in F. S. Regs., Part II. and the Staff Manual respectively. Title pages will be prepared in manuscript.

Place	Date	Hour	Summary of Events and Information	Remarks and references to Appendices
FAVREUIL (SHEET 57C.N.W.) 1/20000	3/8/17	8.30 p.m	After a few days in rest the Bn was ordered to relieve the 2/6" West York Regt in the NOREUIL SECTOR. The B'n left 3 Camp FAVREUIL at 8.30 pm and marched to NOREUIL via VAULX.	
NOREUIL (SHEET 57C.NW) 1/20.000	4/8/17	1.20 am	The relief of the 2/6" Bn was satisfactorily completed by 1.20am 4/8/17 and without casualties. "B" Coy were in support on the SUNKEN ROAD running due south to C16c. The remaining 3 Companies garrisoned the front line HOBART TRENCH with "A" Coy on the right - "C" Coy in the Centre and "D" Coy on the left. Bn line ran from C5.d 55-65 to approximately the NOREUIL - QUEANT ROAD at C10.d 15-6. Bn Headquarters were sited in the SUNKEN ROAD at C10.c 6-9 (ICCAREE CORNER). The 184th Bde 16/8 were on our right + the 2/7 B Durham on our left.	
- do -	7/8/17		The B'n has been employed in during in front of the forward posts every night. On the night 7/8" August a patrol of the Officer and 2 other ranks went out from C.10.c.20 and proceeded along the ridge running eastwards to the RAILWAY. No enemy patrol was encountered so the patrol returned.	
- do -	8/8/17		The Bn has been out during again during the night 8/9 August. Another patrol of one Officer and 2 other ranks went out from C.10.c.20 took the same route as the	

Army Form C. 2118.

WAR DIARY
or
INTELLIGENCE SUMMARY.
(Erase heading not required.)

2/6 Bn. Duke of Wellington's Regt.

Place	Date	Hour	Summary of Events and Information	Remarks and references to Appendices
NOREUIL (SHEET 57C NW) 1/20,000	6/8/17 8/8/17		Previous night this patrol did not encounter any hostile patrol but observed the East Pun Yon Boche Salvary Sct. about 400/500 x from their own wire with our unestablished wire running towards the Boche Lines. This was fallen up and brought back.	
do -	- do -	10:5 p.m.	An S.O.S. signal was sent up by the 2/5th Duke of Wellington who were on our extreme left resulting in the Left NOREUIL SECTOR. This was sent up in response to a retaliating German Boche barrage.	
- do -	9/8/17.		Lieut-Colonel Ford having returned to take over - Major L. Coope 2/4th Yorks & Lancs arrived to take over command of the Bn. Up to the present the time has been quiet and no casualties suffered. The Bn has been engaged in wiring - improving trenches + digging new posts and patrolling. The Earth Pin discovered by the patrol on the 8/8/17 has proved on examination to be the projectile of the German Cable Thrower (KABELWERFER) The maximum range is 492 yards.	Copy of Lieut Colonel Ford's farewell letter attached. See
- do -	12/8/17		Time has been occupied in improving trenches, wiring - making 7 improving posts A patrol was sent out to the CRATERS at C.12.b.2.5 and observed that 3 showed signs of recent work. No hostile patrols were met with.	
FAVREUIL (SHEET 57C NW) 1/20,000	13/8/17.		The Bn. was relieved by the 2/5th York & Lancs Regt. on the night 12/13th August	see

T2134. Wt. W708-776. 500000. 4/15. Sir J. C. & S.

WAR DIARY
or
INTELLIGENCE SUMMARY

Army Form C. 2118.

2/6th Duke of Wellington's Regt

Place	Date	Hour	Summary of Events and Information	Remarks and references to Appendices
FAVREUIL (SHEET 57C NW) 1/20,000	13/8/17		The relief being satisfactorily completed by 1am 13/8/17. After the relief the Bn proceeded to FAVREUIL under cover of 10a.3.0 the total casualties in the line being one NCO slightly wounded. For copy of Operation Orders see appendix.	See
-do-	14/8/17		The Bn struck camp at H.10.a.3.0 and moved into a hutted camp at H.10.c.1.5 where training was continued.	See
-do-	15/8/17		The following were authorised by Div Letter A/5304/3 14/8/17 "Capt N.H.ENGLAND to be Act/g Major whilst employed as Major in 2/8th D of W.	See
BULLECOURT 24/8/17 (SHEET 57 C NW)			20th July, 1917.	See
FAVREUIL (SHEET 57 C NW) 1/20,000	18/8/17		The silver cup for the Best Officer Charger was won by Lt. F.O.Mackellop 2/6 Bn Duke of Wellington Regt at the VI Corps Horse Show held at BIHUCOURT on the afternoon of the 18th August	See
-do-	20/8/17		The Bn has been training and improving new quarters at H.10.c.1-5. Reinforcements of 3 Officers 81 OR arrived for the Bn.	See

Army Form C. 2118.

2/6th Duke of Wellington's Regt

WAR DIARY
or
INTELLIGENCE SUMMARY.
(Erase heading not required.)

Instructions regarding War Diaries and Intelligence Summaries are contained in F.S. Regs., Part II. and the Staff Manual respectively. Title pages will be prepared in manuscript.

Place	Date	Hour	Summary of Events and Information	Remarks and references to Appendices
BULLECOURT. (SHEET 57¼ SW) 1/10 000	2/8/17		The 15th relieved the 2/4th Bn West Yorks Regt. on the Right Subsector of the BULLECOURT SECTOR on the night 20/21st August. The 15th paraded at 7.45 pm and the relief was satisfactorily completed by 1.15 am 21/8/17. The front extended from CHINA LANE (U.22 c 8-15) to the left side of the SUNKEN ROAD at U.23 c 85-053 and the companies were disposed as follows - "A" & "B" Coys on the LEFT, "D" in the Centre & "B" Coy on the Right "C" Coy garrisoned HORSE-SHOE SUPPORT in U.29 c. The Bn H.Q. were on the Rly. CUTTING at U.28 a 9-2.	Copy of operation Orders are attached
do	22/8/17		With the exception of a little hostile T.M. fire the day has been quiet. The Bn have been engaged in improving trenches & C.T. also wiring.	
do	23/8/17		Our front casualties occurred during the night 22/23 a Lewis Team post being struck by a light T.M. shell.	Tel.
do	24/8/17		The day has been quiet. The Battalion has been engaged in improving Trenches and in wiring.	Tel.
do	25/8/17		To date is of special importance occurred during these days. Improvement	Tel.
do	26/8/17		of all parts of line has been pushed forward.	Tel.

Army Form C. 2118.

WAR DIARY
or
INTELLIGENCE SUMMARY. 2/6 Battalion Duke of Wellington's Regt.
(Erase heading not required.)

Instructions regarding War Diaries and Intelligence Summaries are contained in F.S. Regs., Part II. and the Staff Manual respectively. Title pages will be prepared in manuscript.

Place	Date	Hour	Summary of Events and Information	Remarks and references to Appendices
Bullecourt (Sheet 51 B S.W.) 1/10000	27/8/17		Quiet during the day. During the night there were slight skirmishes between patrols in No Man's Land. One slight casualty was sustained by us.	/d/
	28/8/17		The Battalion was relieved by the 1/4 Battalion West Riding Regiment in the Right Sub sector of the Bullecourt Sector during the night. The relief was satisfactorily completed by 11.50 p.m. The Battalion then proceeded to ECOUST. Company Orders were disposed as follows. "A" and "B" Coys occupied Sunken Road C.3.C.2.2. to No.6 C.9 & B.0.5. "C" Coy occupied RAILWAY RESERVE U.27.D.7.3 "D" Coy occupied RAILWAY RESERVE U.28.D. Battalion Head quarters was situated in the Vaults of ECOUST-ST-MEIN C.2.a.7.1.	Copy of Operation Orders attached. /d/
ECOUST (Sheet 57 N.W.)	29/8/17		The Battalion supplied Working Parties for improving and deep breaking Trenches — for making dug outs & for examining Etc under the direction of R.E's. in the Bullecourt Sector.	/d/
	30/8/17		No important event occurred. The Battalion supplied the usual working parties	/d/
	31/8/17		for work on the defences under the direction of R.E. & Coy. On the night of the 31st a small draft of 80 o.r. rejoined the Battalion.	/d/

Rawes Heysham Major
For M.O. Com. 2/6 B. Duke of Wellington's Regt.

SECRET.

WAR DIARY

OF

2/6TH BN DUKE OF WELLINGTON'S REGT.

VOLUME 8.

FROM SEPT 1ST 1917.
TO SEPT 30TH 1917.

Army Form C. 2118.

WAR DIARY
or
INTELLIGENCE SUMMARY.
(Erase heading not required.)

2/4 Battalion Duke of Wellington's (Regiment)

Place	Date	Hour	Summary of Events and Information	Remarks and references to Appendices
ECOUST (Sheet 57 C N.W.)	1/9/17 to 4/9/17		No events of importance occurred. The Battalion was engaged in the wire working parties of a Battalion in support, under the supervision of the R.E.	N.K.S
	5/9/17 to 6/9/17		The Battalion was relieved during the night of the 5th/6th by the 1/4th Battalion K.O.Y.L.I.S. in the left BULLECOURT SECTION SUPPORT AREA. The Battalion was relieved at 12.5 A.M. without casualties, and proceeded to "B"camp, Favreuil H10 C.3.4.	
FAVREUIL SHEET. 57 C N.W.	7/9/17 to 8/9/17 9/9/17.		The Battalion was engaged in training. also carried working parties. Supplies were supplied under orders from the Brigade.	
			The Battalion attended the Brigade Church Parade in the morning. During the remainder of the day the Battalion kept holiday.	
	10/9/17		One Company of the Battalion paraded at the Divisional Gas School during the morning to have all Gas Helmets and Respirators tested. The remainder of the Battalion were engaged in the usual training.	
	11/9/17		In the morning the Battalion including the Bugle Band and	

Army Form C. 2118.

WAR DIARY
or
INTELLIGENCE SUMMARY.

(Erase heading not required.)

1/6 Battalion Duke of Wellingtons Regiment

Instructions regarding War Diaries and Intelligence Summaries are contained in F. S. Regs., Part II. and the Staff Manual respectively. Title pages will be prepared in manuscript.

Place	Date	Hour	Summary of Events and Information	Remarks and references to Appendices
FAVREUIL SHEET. 57c NW.	11/9/17		1st line Transport took part in the Brigade Route March. The Brigade marched from B Camp, FAVREUIL to BIHUCOURT then towards BEHAGNIES by way of GOMIECOURT, then to MORY and back to B Camp. The whole distance being about 7½ miles	
	12/9/17		The Battalion was engaged in the usual training. During the evening the Battalion held Company Cross Country Run which was held. The course was about three miles long, A Company team coming in first.	do
	13/9/17		During the day the Battalion was engaged in cleaning up the Camp prior to going up in the line. On the night of the 13/14 th the Battalion relieved the 2/6 th West Yorks in the Left Sub-section of the Right (NOREUIL) Sector. B and C Companies occupied the front line with A and D Companies in support. The Relief was completed by 2.30 a.m. the casualties for the Battalion being 4, of these three were slight.	do

WAR DIARY
or
INTELLIGENCE SUMMARY.

Army Form C. 2118.

1/6 Battalion Duke of Wellington's Regiment.

Place	Date	Hour	Summary of Events and Information	Remarks and references to Appendices
NOREUIL SHEET	14/9/17		The Battalion was engaged on the usual Trench Routine. During the day the enemy was very active with Trench Mortar fire and we had the following casualties. 2 men wounded.	M.
	15/9/17		No events of any importance happened, the Battalion was subjected to Trench Mortar on the post and support line, two men being wounded.	M.
	16/9/17		During the night D Company relieved a Company of the 7th York & Lanc L Coy. on HORSE SHOE REDOUBT - L.Z.9.c. A Company occupied the whole of PUDSEY SUPPORT. The Battalion had the following casualties 13 wounded. 1 killed and 1 missing.	M.
	17/9/17		On the night of the 17/18th the following inter-company relief took place. A Company relieved B Company in the front line and D Company relieved C Company in the front line. During the 24 hours the casualties to the Battalion were 3 wounded. The Battalion H.Q. were heavily shelled from 3.0 t 4.30 am	M.

Army Form C. 2118.

WAR DIARY
or
INTELLIGENCE SUMMARY.
(Erase heading not required.)

1/6 Battalion Duke of Wellington's Regiment

Place	Date	Hour	Summary of Events and Information	Remarks and references to Appendices
NOREUIL SHEET 57C NW	15/9/17 to 26/9/17		No events of any importance. The Battalion was engaged on holding and improving the position. Two War Dogs were attached to the Battalion as messengers. On the night of the 21st the Battalion was relieved by the 2/7th Duke of Wellington Regt and went into Reserve at IGGAREE CORNER. (C.10.a.6.0). The relief was completed by 10-30pm. without any casualties.	1.
	26/9/17 to 29/9/17		The Battalion was engaged on supplying working parties under the R.E. supervision. On the night of the 26th a draft of 1 Officer and 54 O.R. joined the Battalion. On the night 27/28. The Battalion was relieved by the 2/5 K.O.Y.L.I. in reserve position & and went into Brigade Reserve at the P.O.S. Camp K.27.B.3.1.2. completed by 10-30pm. The Battalion returned the MILITARY MEDAL to honors in the field.	
PAVREUIL 57CNW	30/9/17		266906 Pte Samuel Wilde was awarded the MILITARY MEDAL for bravery in the field Sept 16/17 = 1917. 30th a afternoon there was an Line to Brigade spent the day in cleaning up and inspection.	G.S.

Owen Clayton
Major
Comg 1/6 Bn D of W's R.

SECRET

Vol 10

WAR DIARY

OF

2/6TH BN DUKE OF WELLINGTON'S REG'T

VOLUME 9

FROM OCT 1ST 1917   TO OCT 31ST 1917

Army Form C. 2118.

2/6 Bn DUKE OF WELLINGTON'S REGT

WAR DIARY
or
INTELLIGENCE SUMMARY.
(Erase heading not required.)

Instructions regarding War Diaries and Intelligence Summaries are contained in F.S. Regs., Part II. and the Staff Manual respectively. Title pages will be prepared in manuscript.

Place	Date	Hour	Summary of Events and Information	Remarks and references to Appendices
FAVREUIL (SHEET 57C NW) 1/20,000	1/10/17		The Battalion continued training in No. 5 Camp, FAVREUIL. saw the afternoon a football match was played versus the 2/4th Bn Duke of Wellingtons on the 13th Football Ground, the Bn losing by 3 goals to nil.	
do.	3/10/17		A Football Match was played versus the 2/3rd M.G. Coy & was played away, the 13th winning by one goal to nil.	
do	4/10/17		A Battalion cross country run took place. The starting point being 7th No. 5 Camp FAVREUIL via BIHUCOURT – BIEFVILLERS & then home to No. 5 Camp. Major N.A. ENGLAND proceeded to ENGLAND to attend a three months Course of Gunnery at ALDERSHOT. Pte CHESTER and Pte HAYHURST both won the Boxing Contests at the Brigade Elimination Contest held at FAVREUIL for the VI Corps Winter Sports.	
do	6/10/17		The 13th relieved the 2/5th Bn K.O.Y.L.I. in reserve in the Right NOREUIL Section.	
NOREUIL SHEET 57c NW 51b SW 1/20,000	8/10/17		The Bn paraded at 6 p.m. & proceeded to NOREUIL via BEUGNATRE and VAULX. Bn Headquarters were at IGGAREE CORNER (C10a.5.0) and the Companies were disposed as follows: A Coy at IGGAREE CORNER (C10a.6-9). B Coy in RAILWAY RESERVE at C5d.2-8. "C" Coy in the NOREUIL–LONGATTE RD at	

T2134. Wt. W708—776. 500000. 4/15. Sir J.C. & S.

WAR DIARY
or
INTELLIGENCE SUMMARY.

(Erase heading not required.)

Army Form C. 2118.

2/5 Bn. King's (Liverpool) Regt.

Place	Date	Hour	Summary of Events and Information	Remarks and references to Appendices
— do —	10/10/17		"D" Coy in DEWSBURY - TRENCH (C10b - C11a). The relief was satisfactorily completed by 10.35 p.m. 9/10/17. During the time the 13th were in Reserve - work was carried on under R.E. Super-vision in trenches and dugouts. A Wiring Party was supplied each night for the APEX. (V29d&b).	Nil.
FAVREUIL (SHEET 57c N.W.) 1/20,000	11/10/17		The 13th were relieved by the 4th Bn. ROYAL FUSILIERS, on the night 10/11th October. The relief being satisfactorily completed by 11.35 p.m. 10th October. The 13th proceeded to No. 5 Camp, FAVREUIL. The casualties during the period the 13th were in reserve were nil. Five more Officers arrived as reinforcements were taken on the strength of the 13th.	See Appendix. Copy of O.O. No. 39. Nil.
BEAULENCOURT (SHEET 57c S.W.) 1/20,000	12/10/17		The 13th relieved the 8th Bn. EAST YORKS. REGT in the Hutted Camp at BEAULENCOURT (N18c7.1) &c. on the 12th Oct. The Bn. paraded at 1 p.m. and proceeded to their new quarters near BAPAUME - the cross Roads H28a1-3 being the starting Point. The 13th reached camp about 3.15 p.m. 12/10/17. The Camp vacated by us at FAVREUIL was taken over by the 2nd Bn. ROYAL SCOTS (3rd DIVISION)	See Appendix.

T2134. Wt. W708—776. 500000. 4/15. Sir J.C. & S.

Army Form C. 2118.

2/6 Bn Duke of Wellingtons Regt

WAR DIARY
or
INTELLIGENCE SUMMARY.
(Erase heading not required.)

Place	Date	Hour	Summary of Events and Information	Remarks and references to Appendices
BEAUCOURT (Ref 57c. SW. 1/20,000)	13/10/17		Boxing Tournament were arranged to take place in the evening at Drury Lane Theatre BAPAUME. Between Pte GIBBS. 12th DUBLIN FUSILIERS and 2nd Air Mechanic MILLS R.F.C. No 26566D Pte HAYHURST J. 2/6th Bn Duke of Wellingtons won fastest by Pte GIBBS on points after 4 rounds. 1st Pte CHESTER H beat 2nd Air Mechanic GIBBS. R.F.C. in the 1st Round with a knock-out blow. The Bn has been engaged in Intensive field training during the week. All Officers of the Brigade attended a short series given by Major-Gen I.P. BRAITHWAITE C.B. G.O.C. 62nd Division at the Y.M.C.A. BEAULEY COURT.	Smith / Sgt
— do —	17/10/17		Another Boxing Tournament were arranged to take place at DRURY-LANE THEATRE. BAPAUME. Pte HAYHURST J. again lost to Pte GIBBS on points after 4 rounds. Pte CHESTER H beat 3rd LOWTHER Scotch R.A.M.C. in the 1st Round with a knock-out blow.	
— do —	21/10/17			
— do —	24/10/17		A football Match was arranged with the 2/5th Bn Duke of Wellingtons Regt. The latter winning by 4 goals to nil.	
— do —	26/10/17		The following Honours and Rewards appeared in 62nd Div. Orders dated 26th October 1917 :-	

WAR DIARY
or
INTELLIGENCE SUMMARY.
(Erase heading not required.)

Army Form C. 2118.

2/6 Bn. D. of Welling. Rgt

Place	Date	Hour	Summary of Events and Information	Remarks and references to Appendices
BEAUVOURT (Ref 57° S.W. 1/20,000)	21/10/17		No. 26664 Corporal Thomas Constantine — West Riding Regt. Awarded the Military Medal for marked devotion to duty on the night Sept 19/20th 1917 when in charge of a front line post before Rencourt. (VI Corps R.O. No. 2304 of 25/10/17). No. 266675 Pte James Midgley — West Riding Regt. placed in tend the high appreciation of the gallant conduct of this Bn after a period of intensive training at BEAUVOURT the Bn set out with the Brigade for SIMENCOURT by route march via BATAUME - ACHIET LE GRAND — GOMIECOURT the Bn resting at the latter place for one hour.	
GOMIECOURT (Ref LENS II. 1/10,000)	30/10/17		The Bn proceeded at 5.30 pm. and reached GOMIECOURT about 10.0 pm. the same day where it was accommodated in a tented camp. The Bn paraded at 8.45 a.m. and continued its journey to SIMENCOURT via COURCELLES - RANSART - BEAUMETZ - BEAUMETZ, reaching its destination at 1.45 p.m.	
SIMENCOURT (Ref LENS II. 1/100,000)	31/10/17		the same day — where it entered into occupation of a hutted camp close to the village.	

Secret.   Copy No. 11.
              7/6. Bn. Duke of Wellington's Regt.
                       Order No. 38   6th October 17.
Refer. Sheets 57c. N.W. 1/20.000.
             51b. S.W. 1/20.000.

1. (a) The Battalion will relieve the 7/8th Bn. K.O.Y.L.I. in reserve in the NOREUIL Sector on the night 7/8. October.
   (b) The location of Companies on completion of relief will be:-
   'A' Coy. will relieve 'A' Coy. 7/8. K.O.Y.L.I. at TOGAREE CORNER.
   'B'   -do-   'B' "   -do-   RAILWAY RESERVE C.5.d.
   'C'   -do-   'D' "   -do-   NOREUIL – LONGATTE ROAD
   'D'   -do-   'C' "   -do-   DEWSBURY TRENCH

2. Battalion parade (Fighting Order – Great coats en bandarole) at 6.p.m. The head of the Battalion will pass the VAULX – ST. LEGER ROAD at 7.35.pm. Order of march:- 'B' 'D' 'A' 'C' H.Qrs.

3. Coy. Cmdrs. will arrange to send advance parties to take over stores &c. The following advance party from H.Qrs. will leave No. 5. Camp at 2 p.m. under Lieut. C. SCOTT :- R.S.M., 2 Observers, 3 Signallers and Bombing Sgt.

4. One Limber will accompany each of A.B.C.& D Coys. and 2 will accompany H.Qrs., to carry L/Guns, mess equipment &c.

5. Transport Lines will remain as at present.

6. A duplicate copy of all trench stores taken over will be forwarded to Battn. H.Qrs. by 8. a.m. on the 8th inst.

7. One cook per Coy.   will be left at Wagon Lines.

8. Completion of relief will be reported to Bn. H.Qrs. by the code word "WHITE".

                                W. F. Luckman Capt. & Adjt.
                                7/6. BN. DUKE OF WELLINGTON'S REGT.
Issued at 7 pm.

Copy. No. 1. Retained
      2.   A Coy.
      3.   B "
      4.   C "
      5.   D "
      6.   HQ "
      7.   Q.M.
      8.   T.O.

Copy. No. 9. 2/5 K.O.Y.L.I.
      10. C.O.
      11. Adj.
      12. War Diary
      13.   -do-
      14. File.

10.10.1917

W.F. Luckman
Capt & ?
2/6? Bn Duke of Wellington's Regiment

DISTRIBUTION:

No 1. Copy. H. Qrs Coy.   No 7. Copy - QUARTERMASTER
   2. "   O.C. A. Coy.   8. "   4. Royal Fusiliers
   3. "   " B "   9. "   C.C.
   4. "   " D "   10. "   FILE
   5. "   " C "   11. "   WAR DIARY
   6. "   TRANSPORT OFFICER   12. "   R.S.M.

10/10/17

Duke of Wellington's Regt.

Copy No 15

No. 141. 11/12/16

1. The Battalion will parade in Mass facing East 1 p.m. tomorrow, the 12th inst. Band and drums on the right.
The Head of the Column will pass the starting point – Road junction H. 26. a. 3. 3. – at 1.05 p.m. Route BRESNE – BÉCOURDELENCOURT.

2. Intervals of at least 500 yds. between Battalions and 200 yds. between Companies will be maintained.
1st Line Transport & baggage wagons will march with Units. Echelon "A" will follow immediately in rear of Coys. Echelon "B" & baggage wagons will follow 200 yds in rear of last Coy.

3. Watches will be synchronised with Battn. Signal Office at 11. a.m.

4. O.C. Coys. are responsible that the huts and camp are left in a perfectly clean and sanitary condition. Halts will be made in accordance with Divnl. Coun. Standing Orders Sect. 2. para. 4.

W.J. Luckman Capt. & Adjt.
1/6. Bn. Duke of Wellington's Regiment

Issued at 9. p.m.

To all recipients of Order No. 140.

Duke of Wellington's Regt. Order No 43   Copy No 13
B.E.F.   30th October 1917

1. My Battalion will march to SWANCOURT tomorrow 31st Oct.
   Programme tomorrow:-
        6.30 a.m.   Reveille
        7.15 a.m.   Breakfast
        7 a.m.   Blankets (rolled in bundles of 10 and
                    labelled) Officers' valises, mess equipment &c
                    will be stacked on road outside Camp.
        8.30 a.m.   Battalion Parade
                    Order of march:- H.Qrs. C, D & B Coys.

2. An advance party consisting of 1 N.C.O & 4 men per
   Coy and H.Qrs. will parade at Orderly Room 7.15 a.m.

3. Loading party, as under, will report to Q.M. at 7 a.m.
   1 N.C.O & 7 men "C" Coy. & two details by Q.M.

4. Rear Guard of 1 N.C.O & 10 men "B" Coy will be detailed
   in accordance with B.S. Standing Orders, Section
   para 7. This Guard will march in rear of 105
   Field Ambulance until arrival of transport A/2 will escort
   them forward direct to SWANCOURT.

5. Returns in accordance with B.S. Standing Orders
   will be submitted to Orderly Room immediately
   on arrival in new area.

6. Orders regarding distances to be maintained, Rations &c
   will be as detailed in Order No 42.
   Dinners will be served after arrival in new Camp.

                                W. F. Luckman
                                    Capt & Adj
                        1/6 Bn Duke of Wellington's West Riding Regt.

Dinners at 6 p.m.

Copies not Retained   Copy to be Mobn. Coy   Copy to W. L. Coxe
    2. A Coy   7. Ady. Officer   12. R.S.M.
    3. B Coy   8. Adjt.   13. War
    4. C Coy   9. Q.M.   14. Diary
    5. D Coy   10. T.O.

October 1917

2/6 DUKE OF WELLINGTON'S

WAR DIARY

SECRET

WAR DIARY

OF

2/6TH BN DUKE OF WELLINGTON'S REGT.

VOLUME 10

From Nov 1st 1917.   To Nov 30th 1917

Army Form C. 2118.

WAR DIARY
or
INTELLIGENCE SUMMARY.
(Erase heading not required.)

2/6 DUKE OF WELLINGTONS (W.R.) REGT.

Place	Date	Hour	Summary of Events and Information	Remarks and references to Appendices
SIMENCOURT	1917 Nov 1		Interior Training	
SHEET 51cSE	2		" "	
	3		" "	
	4		Practice attack with Limbers (limbers were used to represent tanks)	
	5		" "	
	6		Officers & Platoon Sgts attended demonstration at WAILLY. The 187 Inf Brigade in practice attack supported by tanks. Bn H.Q. & 4 officers AS. O.R.	
	7		The Battalion carried out a practice attack in co operation with tanks at WAILLY.	
	8		The Sgts held a "Smoking Concert" in their mess. The Battalion carried out a tactical exercise with cavalry aeroplanes in the 9004 area	
	9		Specialist Training	
	10		The Battalion in practice attack.	
	11		Attended Bath at MONCHET Brig Gen. F.F. Hill C.B. CMG DSO for the Bath farewell & goodluck	
	12		Interior Economy	

Army Form C. 2118.

WAR DIARY
or
INTELLIGENCE SUMMARY.
(Erase heading not required.)

2/6 DUKE OF WELLINGTONS (W.R.) REGT.

Instructions regarding War Diaries and Intelligence Summaries are contained in F.S. Regs., Part II. and the Staff Manual respectively. Title pages will be prepared in manuscript.

Place	Date	Hour	Summary of Events and Information	Remarks and references to Appendices
	1917			
	Nov. 13		The Battalion marched from SIMENCOURT to ACHIET-LE-PETIT. En tents & Bivs at Bradford Camp.	
ACHIET LE PETIT.	14		Brig Gen R.B. Bradford V.C. M.C. introduced himself to the Battalion as the new Brig of the 186 Inf Brigade.	
SHEET 57C	15		The Battalion was reorganised for the usual training.	
			186 Brigade Football League. 2/6 Dukes v Wellington. 1/6 W Ridg. v 5 whr washington. 1 goal.	
	16	9 AM	The Battalion attended Divine Service at the Cinema.	
		11:30AM	Football Match. N.C.Os 4 goals Officers 2 goals.	
		7:30 PM	The Battalion marched to LITTLE WOOD BATTN CAMP YTRES, arriving there	
			at 2 AM on the morning of the 17 inst	
			A draft consisting of 1 Officer + 219 O.R. joined the Battalion at YTRES	
			at 4 PM	
YTRES.	17	11:15 AM	The C.O. spoke to men on forthcoming operations	
SHEET 57C		5:30 PM	The C.O. spoke to Coy Commanders	
SPECIAL MAP	18	9 AM	The C.O. + Coy Cmdrs visited the line + made reconnaissance K32 - Q4	
MOEUVRES		4 PM	The Battalion marched to BERTINCOURT.	
	19	5:30 AM	The Batt. left BERTINCOURT + marched to assembly position in HAVRINCOURT WOOD	

Army Form C. 2118.

WAR DIARY
or
INTELLIGENCE SUMMARY.

(Erase heading not required.)

2/6 DUKE OF WELLINGTONS (W.R.) REGT.

Place	Date	Hour	Summary of Events and Information	Remarks and references to Appendices
	1917			
SPECIAL MAP	Nov 20	6.20AM	The 62 Division attacked the German lines from Q4.b.7.6 to the CANAL DU NORD	
MOEUVRES			The 185 Brigade on the Right & 187 Brigade on the Left, 186 Brigade in Support.	
			The first objective was from CANAL at K20 d.2.1 - K21 N.6.2 - K22 c.3.2 (Junction of SUNKEN ROAD & RAILWAY) & along the RAILWAY to K23 a.4.2. This line was very soon reached with very few casualties the cooperation of Tanks made this quite easy. MOEUVRES fell into our hands without along much resistance. The second objective was from CANAL in K15 c.2.9 - K15 b.4.2 (X Roads) along road to K16 c.4.9 - K16 b.0.3 - K16 b.4.5 to SUNKEN ROAD at K17 a.7.5. The charging forth at K17 c was included. This line soon fell into our hands & a large number of prisoners were taken.	
			The 186 Brigade went forward & took up a jumping off position on this line. The Battalion took up a position from CANAL K15 c.2.9 to K16 A.4.5 & immediately swept forward. The ground attacked & won by the Battalion was as follows. LOCK No 6 of CANAL in K3a HUGHES SUPPORT in K3a - K3d - K3d, along SUNKEN ROAD K4c & K4d to K4d 5.5. HINDENBURG SUPPORT TRENCH running from K16 b.4.5 - K3d - K10 b to K4d 5.5. The attack was a complete success & 2 Officers & 165 men, 1 Battery of 5.9 Now	

WAR DIARY or INTELLIGENCE SUMMARY.

Army Form C. 2118.

2/6 DUKE OF WELLINGTON'S (W.R.) REGT.

(Erase heading not required.)

Instructions regarding War Diaries and Intelligence Summaries are contained in F.S. Regs., Part II. and the Staff Manual respectively. Title pages will be prepared in manuscript.

Place	Date	Hour	Summary of Events and Information	Remarks and references to Appendices
	1917			
SPECIAL MAP	Nov. 20		1 Battery 9.77mm Field guns. 1 Light Trench Mortar + 1 Machine gun were captured + 10 Machine guns were destroyed along with their crews	
MOEUVRES			At the same time the 2/4 D.G.W. had formed + took GRAINCOURT. The Battalion held their position through the night	
	21		On this day the enemy again in E17 – E18 – E19 was attacked by the Brigade + the Battalion was B Junct. on T of the attack was unsuccessful + later the Trench mornings N of BOURLON in E12 – E11 – E11. The attack however was held up + the Battalion reinforced the other Batt. in SUNKEN ROAD E17/6 – E23d – E24d. + the Trench – E23d. 9.1 + E14 35.45. This time was held until the Brigade was relieved by the 185 Inf. Brigade. When relieved the Battalion went into support in dug outs at K4.b.35 in SUNKEN ROAD to K5.c.14. 2/Lt Wright was killed + Lt. Stroker + Lt. Reed slightly wounded.	
	22		The Battalion was still in support	
	23	7AM	The Battalion moved BB + went into billets at BERTINCOURT	
	24		The C.O. congratulated the Batt. on its magnificent performance. The casualties were:- Officers 1 killed 2 slightly wounded. O.R. 15 killed 61 wounded 4 missing	

Army Form C. 2118.

WAR DIARY
or
INTELLIGENCE SUMMARY.
(Erase heading not required.)

2/6 DUKE OF WELLINGTONS (W.R.) REGT.

Instructions regarding War Diaries and Intelligence Summaries are contained in F. S. Regs., Part II. and the Staff Manual respectively. Title pages will be prepared in manuscript.

Place	Date	Hour	Summary of Events and Information	Remarks and references to Appendices
	1917.			
	Nov. 24		During the operations of the preceding days the 36 Division operated on the Left & the 51 Division on the Right.	out
	25	1.30 PM	The Battalion left BERTINCOURT & relieved the elements of the 119 Inf Brigade 40 Division in BOURLON WOOD at dusk. The Line taken over was E12.a.9.9 – F.13.c.1.4 – F.7.d.2.3.6. During the night 2 strong posts were constructed at E.12.d.5.0 & F.7.c.4.2.	out
	26		The Battalion worked very hard & dug quite a good line. At 4.30 PM the enemy put up a machine gun barrage & shelled the WOOD for 1½ hours.	out
	27	6.20 AM	The Brigade attacked the enemy position having the RAILWAY from F.12.3.7 to F.2.c.0.3 as its objective. The 139 Inf Brigade were on the Left & the Guards Division on the Right. The 2/8 West Yorks were attached to 186 Brigade for the operation. The Batt attacked & took BOURLON but further progress was not possible under the Lift or Right flanks. The village was not supported either on the Left or Right flanks. The village was held until 5 P.M. when the Batt retired & took up a position in BOURLON WOOD on the rear. This position covered the village & 92th Field of fire.	out

Army Form C. 2118.

WAR DIARY
or
INTELLIGENCE SUMMARY.
(Erase heading not required.)

2/6 DUKE OF WELLINGTONS (W.R.) REGT.

Instructions regarding War Diaries and Intelligence Summaries are contained in F.S. Regs., Part II and the Staff Manual respectively. Title pages will be prepared in manuscript.

Place	Date	Hour	Summary of Events and Information	Remarks and references to Appendices
	1917			
SPECIAL	MARCH 27		Was relieved. During the day the enemy shelled BOURLON WOOD with very heavy guns thereby causing many casualties. 21 Sergeants and Captain during this attack. At dusk the battalion was relieved by Somerset & Oxfordy including Sgts. Jenks, 3 Hancows & 15 Sergeants + Sergeant + Capt. S.W. John'n the WOOD. Capt. B.S. Mann, Lieut F.S. Holland, 2nd Lieut B. S. Holland, 2nd Lieut H.J. Clarkson were killed + Capt R. Somerville, Capt. N.T. Howell, 2Lieut M. Irwin, 2Lieut F.J. Humphreys were wounded. 28 Other Ranks were killed - 137 Wounded + Missing.	
MOEUVRES	28		The enemy continued to shell the WOOD. 2nd of Wellington's all 8 P.M. by the 141 Inf. Brigade. 147 Division + 141st. I.B.	
	29		Yrcles. RQC	
	30		Brigadier General R.B. Bradford V.C. Mc. was killed. 2/6 Duke of Wellington's took command of the Brigade.	
	DEC 1.		The Batt moved from RQC to dig a line of posts from M.42.b.73 to K.6.b.0.4.4. These posts were reinforced by night + during the day the Battn stayed in the old British line in K.9.b.	

SECRET (ORIGINAL)

WAR DIARY

OF

2/6th BN DUKE OF WELLINGTON'S REGT

VOLUME II

FROM 1st DEC 1917 — To 31st DEC 1917

WAR DIARY or **INTELLIGENCE SUMMARY**

Army Form C. 2118.

2/6 DUKE OF WELLINGTONS (W.R.) REGT.

Place	Date	Hour	Summary of Events and Information	Remarks and references to Appendices
	1917			
SPECIAL MAP	Dec. 2		The Batt. stayed in Old British lines in KMd by day & occupied the line of posts	
MOEUVRES			by night K9a.m.3 - K3a.4.7	S.W.1
	3		The Batt. moved to BEAUMETZ-LES-CAMBRAI & stayed in tents	S.W.1
	4		Marched to FREMICOURT & entrained. Detrained at BEAUMETZ-LES-LOGES & marched	
	5		to BAILLEULVAL	S.W.7
LENS.	5		Marched to GOUVES & took over billets from 1/1 R.F. LONDON REGT.	D.W.Y
	6		Marched to TINCQUES. XIII Corps Area 1 Army	S.W.1
	7		The Batt. attended the faths in TINCQUES	S.W.1
	8		Football Matches were played by Coys.	S.W.1
	9		The Batt. paraded for Divine Service, which was held in the CINEMA	S.W.1
HAZEBROUCK 5A	10		Marched to LAPUGNOY	S.W.1
	11		Coys held inspections of kit etc	W.1
	12		Training	S.W.
	13		"	S.W.
	14		The Batt. marched to SONNEHEM	S.W.
	15		Football Match 2/6 Duke of Wellingtons 5 goals 2/4 West Riding Regt. 14?? 1 goal	S.W.

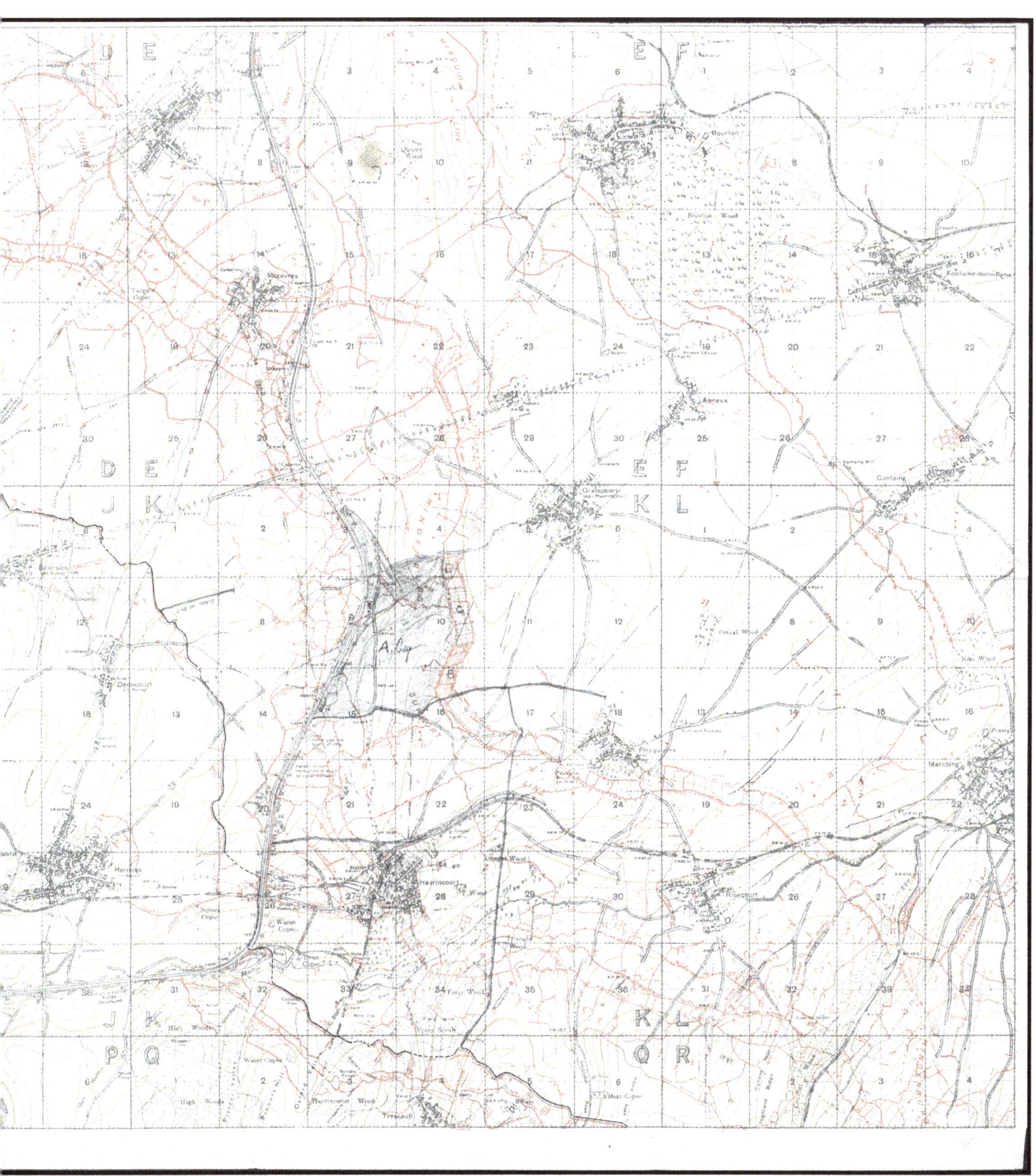

2/6 Duke of Wellingtons

War Diary

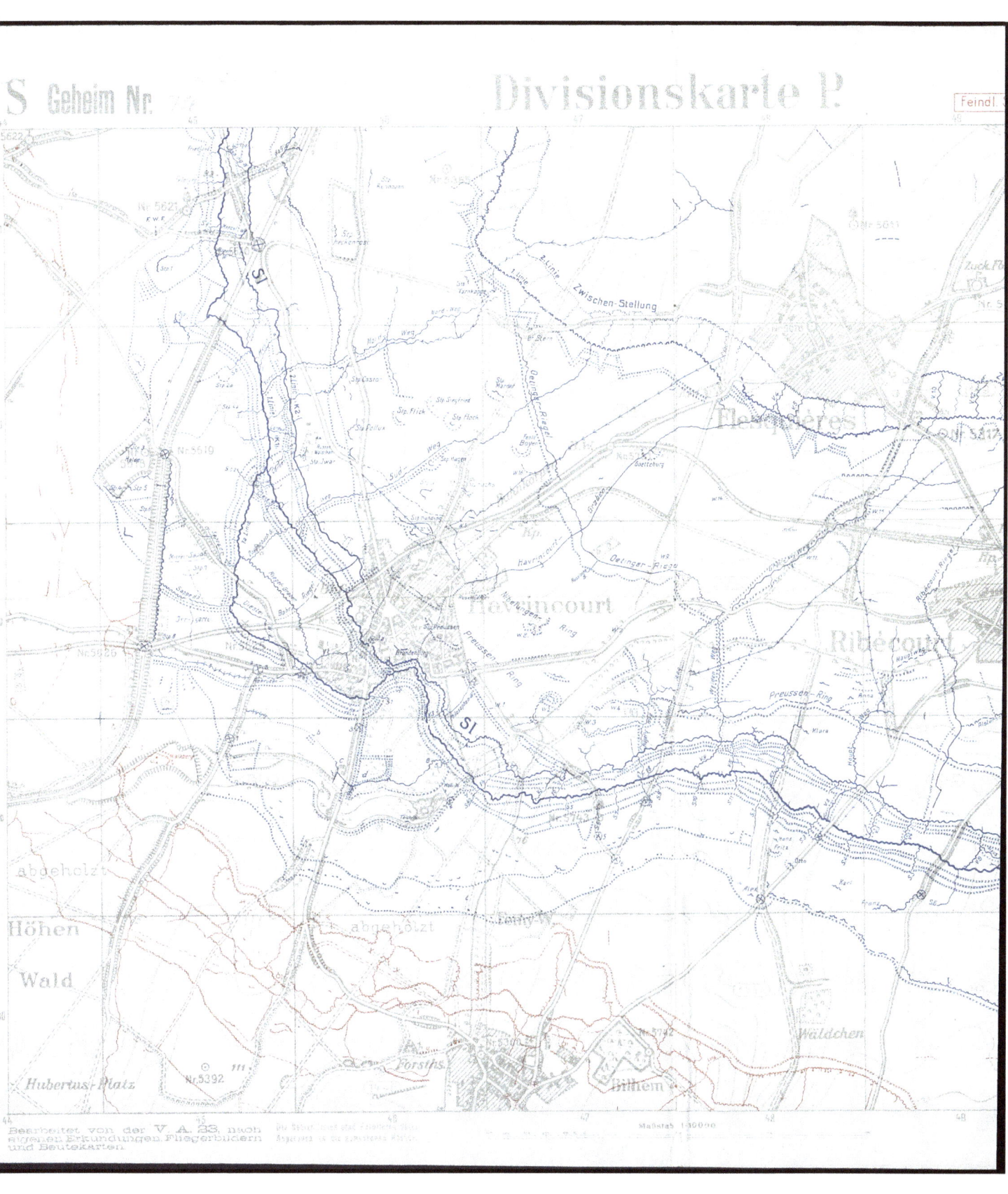

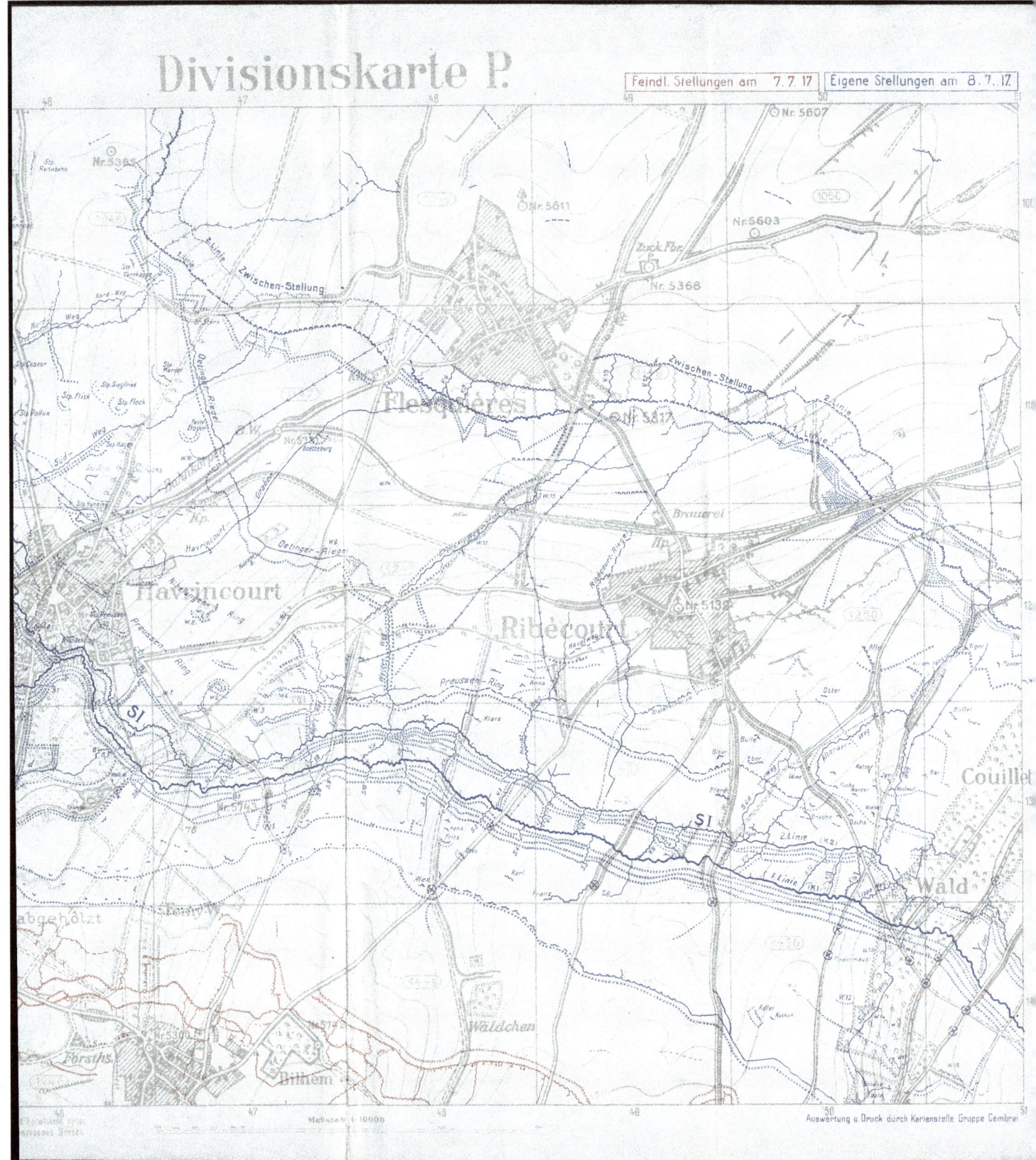

2/6 DUKE OF WELLINGTONS

WAR DIARY

(CAPTURED MAP)

2/6

2/6 DUKE OF
WELLINGTONS

WAR DIARY

Army Form C. 2118.

WAR DIARY
or
~~INTELLIGENCE~~ SUMMARY.

2/6 DUKE OF WELLINGTONS (W.R.) REGT.

(Erase heading not required.)

Instructions regarding War Diaries and Intelligence Summaries are contained in F. S. Regs., Part II. and the Staff Manual respectively. Title pages will be prepared in manuscript.

Place	Date	Hour	Summary of Events and Information	Remarks and references to Appendices
	1917			
HAZEBROUCK 5A	Dec. 16		Training	S.M.
	17		"	
	18		The Batt. marched to LAPUGNOY	
LENS. 11	19		The Batt. marched to BETHONSART area	
	20		BETHONSART. HQ. A, B, C, Coys billeted in VILLERS BRULIN	
	21		The Batt. carried out a system of training	
	22		"	
	23		"	
	24		"	
	25		The C.O. treated all Coys during dinner. The officers dined together at (?)	
	26		Gave a hot dinner to the men. w.k.	
	26		Training. The Sgts held a Smoking Concert	
	27		Football Match 4/6 D.L.W. 14 goals, 2/6 D.W.R. 1 goal	
	28		Training	
	29		Practice attack with 213 M.G.C.	

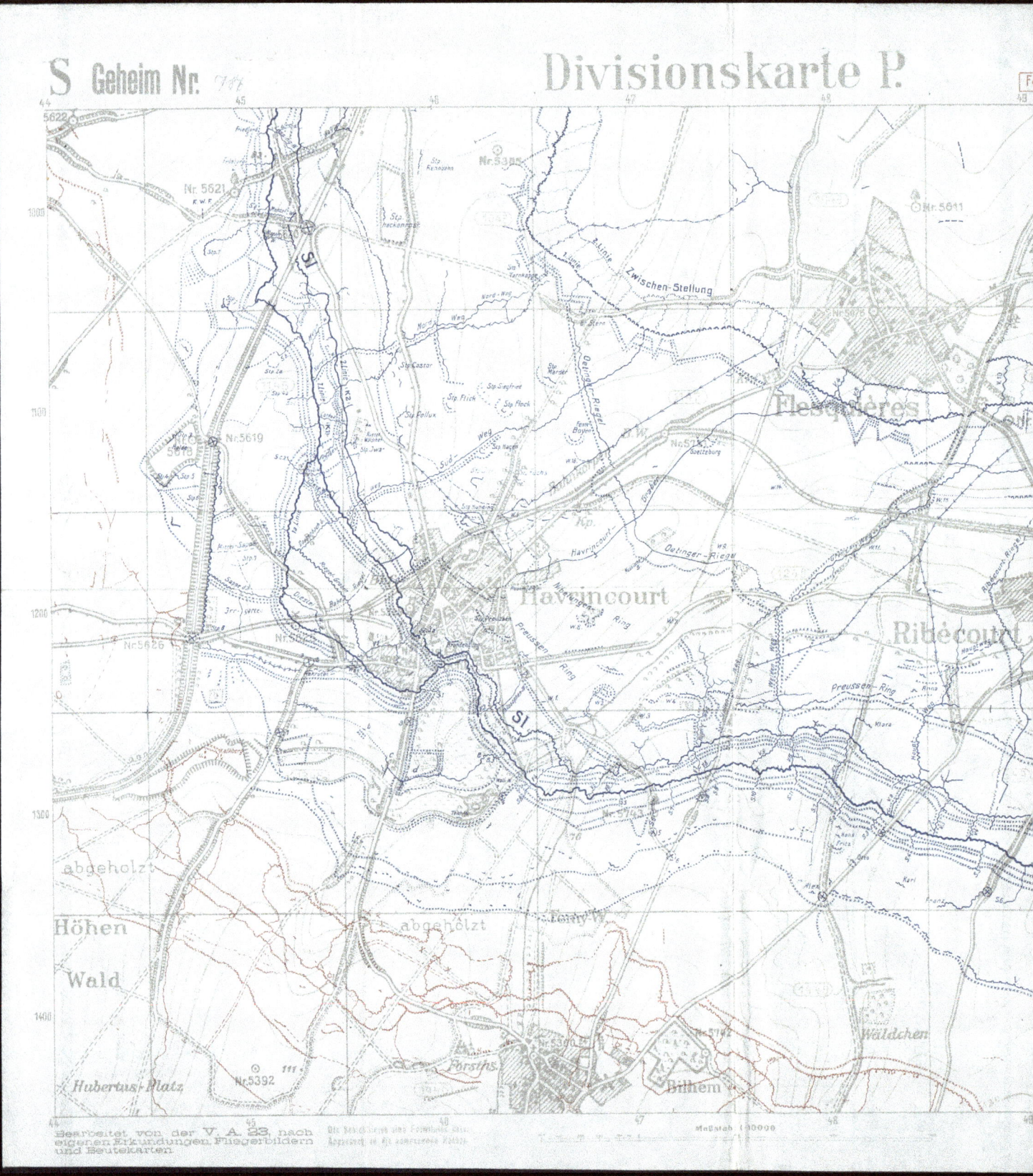

2/6 DUKE OF WELLINGTONS.

WAR DIARY

(CAPTURED MAP)

Original

Army Form C. 2118.

WAR DIARY
or
INTELLIGENCE SUMMARY.

2/6 DUKE OF WELLINGTON'S (W.R.) REGT.

(Erase heading not required.)

Place	Date	Hour	Summary of Events and Information	Remarks and references to Appendices
LENS II	1917 Dec 30		Services were held in the school. VILLERS BRULIN	SM
	31		The Batt. marched to Battns at TINCQUES	SM

H. Bromley Lt.Col.

Comdg 2/6 Bn Duke of Wellington Regt.

"A" Form.
MESSAGES AND SIGNALS.

TO: 2/4 D of W (struck through)
2/5 D of W.

Sender's Number: B1726
Day of Month: 1

AAA

Batt^n will move tonight & dig a line of posts on general line K6.b.8½.9. through K8.a & K7.b to K7.a.8.3. 2/4 on the right 2/5th on the left aaa Dividing line about K8.a.4.7. Capt Bruce will meet unit representatives at Bge HQrs at 5 pm. Units must salve tools at once.

From: 186th

O 1/4 D. of W. Regt.   Bgde/C/4
1/6 do

(1) Picks and shovels have now arrived at the crossing over the Canal 100 yards South of Lock 7 (K.15.a.4.6.)

Battalions will proceed forthwith to the above point where they will draw the tools required and will be led by their Company Guides to meet Captain BRUCE at the Assembling Point K.8.a.4.7.

Battalions will each draw 10 tins of S.O.S. Grenades at the same point as the tools.

2 men per Battalion will report to Lieut. SMITHSON for this purpose.

(2) Work on the Line of Posts will cease before dawn and Battalions will occupy positions during the day as under:-

1/4 D of W. Regt. the Trenches on the N.W. Portion of K.9.a.
1/6 do. the Trenches in neighbourhood of K.9 central.

(3) ACKNOWLEDGE
1.12.17 9.15/- E.W. Hereford Captain
                   186 Inf. Bde.

Secret.   Copy No. 3

186th INFANTRY BRIGADE
OPERATION ORDER No. 69.

1st December 1917.

(1) The situation on 2nd Division front remains generally unchanged. The enemy have been reported massing this morning in K.16.a and b. and are being dealt with by our Artillery.

(2) The 1/7 D. of W. Regt. will be prepared to move at short notice to take up a position in the HINDENBURG LINE (E.26.d) and the trench in E.25.b. and to connect up these two trenches with a line of POSTS from E.26.c.1.8. to E.26.d.0.8.

The 1/5 D. of W. Regt. will be prepared to occupy the HINDENBURG LINE in K.3.a and K.2.b.

The above positions are at present occupied by the 22nd ROYAL FUSILIERS 99th INF BDE. attached to 5 INF Bde.

(2)

Their Headquarters are in the HINDENBURG LINE immediately North of the BAPAUME - CAMBRAI Road in E 26 d.

(3) The 1/5 and 1/7 D. of W's Rgts. will send Officers forthwith to reconnoitre these positions and will report to Brigade Headquarters when the reconnaissance is completed.

(4) ~~ACKNOWLEDGE.~~

Time of issue 11:30 a.m.

Captain
Brigade Major
146 Inf Brigade.

Copies to
1. O/C 1/4 D. of W.
2. 1/5 do
3. 1/6 do
4. 1/7 do
5. 213 M.G. Coy
6. 146 T.M.B.y

SECRET   Copy No 3.

186th INFANTRY BRIGADE
OPERATION ORDER No 70.

1st Decr 1917

(1) The 186th INF BDE will take up positions tonight as follows :-

2/7 D of W. Regt Hindenburg Front and Support Trenches in E.26.d North of CAMBRAI-BAPAUME Road from E.26.d.7.3 through E.26.d.5.7. to E.26.d.1.9 with supports in the Hindenburg Front trench from E.26.d.2.1 to E.26.d.1.9, thence line of POSTS from E.26.d.1.9. to E.26.c.1.8 thence along trench to E.25.b.2.4.
Headquarters about E.26.d.2.1.

2/5 D of W. Regt will occupy the Hindenburg Line from LOCK 6 inclusive to E.26.d.7.3. with supports in the Hindenburg front trench from K.3.a.7.3 to E.26.d.2.1.
Headquarters about K.3.a.7.3.

②

1/4 D. of W. Regt will dig and occupy line of POSTS tonight from K.8.b.85.90. along high ground to K.8.a.4.7.
Headquarters about K.8.b.3.1.

1/6 D. of W. Regt will dig and occupy line of POSTS from the LEFT of 1/4 D. of W. Regt. at K.8.a.4.7 to the old BRITISH Line about K.7.a.8.3.
Headquarters about FORK-Roads K.7.d.4.5.

The General Line to be occupied by the 1/4th and 1/6th D. of W. Regt. will be pointed out to Battalion Representatives by a Staff Officer of the Brigade.

213 Machine Gun Coy. will place 6 guns in the most suitable position to protect the line of 1/4th and 1/6th Duke of W. Regt from any attacks from the North and N.E.
Remaining guns of 213 M.G. Coy will be held in Brigade Reserve

(3)

in their present positions.
Brigade Headquarters will
[remain] at LOCK 7.

(2) The 2/5" and 1/7 D. of W. Regt.
will not move to take up their
new positions till receipt of
further Orders from the 186 INF.
BRIGADE.

The 2/4" and 1/6 D. of W. Regt.
will move immediately on
return of Representatives from
Bde HQ

(3) As soon as Battalions
have occupied their new
positions, they will send 2
Runners to Brigade HQ with
report as to their dispositions
and exact locations of
Battalion HQ

(4) ACKNOWLEDGE.

Rifles D.g.m. Regt
  /5   do
  /6   do   ✓   Ref 36/E/12.
  /7   do
 2/13   M.G. Coy
 2/16   ~~M.G. Coy~~

With reference to O.O No 70
the line to be constructed by
the 1/4th and 1/6 D.g.m. Rif.
will be a single line of Posts
to hold about 12 rifles each
and of the shape shown as
under :—

11/186/16 posts   This line of posts must be
                   constructed slightly on the forward
   192   slope in order to be clear of the
                   fire of our own guns which
                   are in the Valley behind.

Battalions will be guided
to the Dividing Point
at K.8.a.4.7. and will
wheel outwards from there at
a bearing of approx 90° magnetic
and 270° magnetic respectively.

4. One NCO of 226th Field Coy RE will be attached to each Battalion to give technical assistance.

Battalions, when ordered to move, will concentrate immediately South of Love 7 where they will draw tools and will then be guided to K.8.a.4.7. by the Company Guides who will have been shown the rendezvous.

G Wingfield Mahood Cayton
Brigade Major
186 Inf. Brigade

1.12.17

10 Ans
SOS

(2)

all Lewis Gun Drums, MG Signals, Petrol Tins, tools etc. in their possessions are brought out with them.

5. On completion of moves, 1/4th and 1/6 Bn of the Regt will be in readiness at 1 hour's notice to move in support of 2nd Division if required.

6. The Staff Captain 185th Inf. Bde, will arrange billeting parties at BEAUMETZ. Transport lines will move to BEAUMETZ.

7. The 213 M.G. Company will remain in its present position under orders of 5th Infantry Brigade.

8. Brigade H.Q. will close at Lock 7 at dusk, and will move to BEAUMETZ.

9. Acknowledge.

G. Wingfield Hartford
Captain
Brigade Major
185 Inf. Brigade

Time of issue:

Copies to 1. 2/4 L.F.   6. R.M.O.
2. 2/5 do   7. 5 Inf. Bde
3. 2/6 do   8. 185 Inf. Bde
4. 2/7 do   9. Signals
5. 213 MGC   10. War Diary

Secret   166 Inf. Bde.   Copy No 3

OPERATION ORDER No 71.

3rd December 1917

1. The 166 Inf Bde (less 213 M.G. Coy.)
    will move today, 3rd inst, to BEAUMETZ.

2. The 2/4th and 2/6th D of W. Regt will
    move by day in small parties of
    not more than 15 men each, and
    at intervals of not less than 200
    yards between parties, this will
    avoid unity in the observation from
    the enemy.
    Units will start moving as under:-
    2/4 2/6 D.of W. Regt } starting at any
    166 M.G.Coy   } time after 10 a.m.
    2/5th and 2/7 D of W. Regt will move
    at dusk.

3. Cook's Limbers for each battalion
    will be sent to Cooks of to
    prepare their tea under:-
    2/4 and 2/6 D of W. Regt 9.30 a.m.
    2/5 and 2/7 D of W. Regt 4.30 p.m.

4. Battalions will carry their

SECRET   Copy No. 3

ADDENDUM No 1 to
1st 2nd Bn. OPERATION ORDER No 71

3rd Dec 1917.

1. The 1/5 and 1/7 D. of W. Regt. will not move from their present positions till relieved by the 17 Royal Fusiliers.

    The 17 Royal Fusiliers will arrive as soon as possible after dusk.

    The 17 Royal Fusiliers will take over the line as under:-

    'D' Coy. — The trenches astride the Sunk Rd. in E.25.b.

    'C' Coy. — Trenches in E.26.c and d. North of BAPAUME – CAMBRAI Rd.

    'A' Coy. — Dugouts. K.3.a.7.3.

    'B' Coy. — Strengthening front line in K.3.a and K.2.b.

    HQ — K.3.a.7.3.

    Companies will arrive in the order shown above.

    1/7 D. of W. Regt. will send 2 guides per company to bring up each of 'D' and 'C' Coys.

    1/5 D. of W. Regt. will send 2 guides per Coy. to bring up each of 'A' and 'B' Coys. and 1 guide for Battalion HQ.

(2)

the 1/5 D. of W. Reg. will also provide a reliable N.C.O. to take charge of all guides.

Guides will report to Brigade H.Q. at Lock 7 by 3.30 pm and will be provided with written instructions as to their destination on the line.

2. At 4 pm till completion of relief by 1 Royal Irish, the 1/5th and 1/7 D. of W. Reg. both come under the Orders of 5th Inf. Brigade.

After relief Battalion will proceed by the most convenient route to COUMETZ

3. 186 Inf. Brigade H.Q. will close at Lock 7 at 4 pm and will re-open at COUMETZ on arrival.

4. Limbers for conveyance of 1/5th and 1/7 D. of W. Reg. Lewis Guns will be at Lock 7 at 4.30 pm as arranged.

(3)

5. ACKNOWLEDGE

Guingand Lt/Col) Captain
) Brigade Major
              86) Inf Brigade

Time of Issue: 1.45 pm

Copies to:-
1. 74 Bde/P. Rt
2. 75   do
3. 76   do
4. 77   do
5. 217 M.G. Coy
6. 186 JM.A
7. 5 Inf. Bde
8. 185 Inf Bde
9. Staff Captain
10. O/C
11. War Diary.

Copy No. 11

2/6. BN. DUKE OF WELLINGTON'S REGT. ORDER No 47

Ref: HAZEBROUCK 5a. 1/40000. 13th Dect. 1917.

1/ The Battalion will move to GONNEHEM tomorrow, 14th Dec. 1917.

2/ The Battalion will parade in Column of Route facing N.E. on the road leading to CHOCQUES, head of the column at 'A' Coy. Officers' billet (No.   ) Order of march H.Qrs. A. B. C. D. & Transport.
Dress:- Marching Order (as demonstrated to C.S.M's. at TINCQUES)
Mounted Officers:- Fighting order.

3/ Lewis gun limbers will follow companies.

4/ Distances of 100 yds. will be maintained between Coys. and between Coys. and transport.

5/ Officers' valises will be stacked as follows:- H.Qrs A & C. Coys. at Bridge, near Orderly Room; remainder in yard at Transport billet, by 8.30. am.
Blankets (tightly rolled in bundles of 10.) mess equipment &c. will be stacked as follows:-
H.Qrs. A. & C. Coys., at bridge near Orderly Room } By
B & D Coy. & Transport at Q.M. Stores } 8. am.

6 One baggage wagon will be loaded at the bridge and one at Transport Yard.

7 'C' Coy. will detail 1. NCO. & 6 men to take charge of the dump at the bridge from 8 am. onwards. This party will act as loading party.
'B' Coy. will detail 1. NCO. & 4 men to report to Q.M. as loading party at 8. am.
The above two parties will proceed on lorries and act as unloading parties at GONNEHEM.
'D' Coy. will detail 1. N.C.O. and 4 men to load baggage wagons at Transport lines at 8.30. am.
This party will return to its coy. immediately after loading Officers' valises.

8 On arrival in new area companies will at once send usual reports to BN. HQrs. at the CHATEAU.

W.H. Luckman
Capt. & Adjt.
2/6. Bn. Duke of Wellington's Regt.

Issued at 5. pm.
Copy. No. 1. C.O.
2-6. Coys & HQ.
7. T.O.
8. Q.M.
9-10. War Diary
11. Retain.

2/6 Bn DUKE OF WELLINGTON'S REG'T. ORDER NO 48   Copy to ___

17 Dec 1917.

1. The Battalion will move to LAPUGNOY on 18 Dec 1917, the same billets will be taken over as were previously occupied.

2. The Battalion will parade at 9.25 am in column of fours in Main St. facing S. Head of Column to be against Transport Lines & order of march & HQrs. A C D A.
Dress - Full Marching Order.
Distances of 100 yds between Coys. & A Coy & Transport will be maintained.

3. Blankets will be rolled in bundles of 10 (tightly) & stacked at QM Stores by 7.30 am.
Officers Valises will be stacked at QM Stores by 8.30 am.

4. OC C Coy will detail a loading party of 1 NCO & 10 men to report at QM Stores at 7.30am & to remain until blankets & valises are loaded.

5. Lorries. Mess equipment &c will be dumped at QM Stores by 7.30 am.

6. Baggage Wagons will report to QM Stores at 7 am.

7. 2/Lt Scott and 8 men Hq Coy will act as rear party, and will ensure that all billets are left scrupulously clean & will without fail obtain clearing certificate from the Town Major — this will be handed in to Orderly Room immediately on arrival in new station.
This party will join the Battalion at LAPUGNOY after obtaining clearing certificate.

8. OC Coys will render to Orderly Room by 8.45am certificates that billets have been left scrupulously clean.

W Shuckman
Capt. Adjt.
2/6 Bn Duke of Wellington's Regt.

Issued at
Copy No. 1. CO.   8. QM.   12. Retain.
       2-6. Coys & Hq   9-10 War Diary   13. Adj
       7. TO.   11. R.S.M.   14. 2/Lt Scott.

2/6 BN. DUKE OF WELLINGTON'S REGT.   ORDER NO. 49.   14

1. The Battalion will move to VILLERS-BRULIN, BETHONSART, GUESTREVILLE tomorrow 19th Decr 1917.
Route:- MARLES-LES-MINES - BRUAY - HOUDAIN - MAGNICOURT.

2. The Battalion will parade at 8 a.m. in column of fours, in Main Street facing S.W. Head of Column to be against Q.M. Stores.
Order of march: H.Qrs. C. D. A. Coys. Transport - B Coy.
Dress:- Fighting Order - Jerkins to be packed in valises with great-coats.
Distances of 100 yds between Coys - & Coys & Transport will be maintained.

3. In view of the frost B Coy. will march in rear of the transport. Transport Officer will have drag-ropes ready for use in case of necessity, also spades to sprinkle any very slippery places with earth. O.C. "B" Coy. will render any necessary assistance.

4. Blankets (rolled tightly, in bundles of 10) men's valises, mess equipment &c. will be stacked at Q.M. Stores by 7. a.m.
B & D. Coy. Officers' valises will be stacked at Q.M. Stores, & H.Q. & C. Coy. Officers' valises at Bridge near Orderly Room, by 7. a.m.

5. O.C. H.Q. Coy. will detail 1 N.C.O. & 4 men to load Baggage Wagon at Bridge at 7. a.m.

6. Lorries (probably 5) will report at Q.M. Stores at 8 a.m.

7. Baggage Wagons will report to Q.M. Stores at 7 a.m.

8. Lieut E.N. Taylor & 5 Hqrs signallers will proceed to new area starting at 6 a.m.

9. The column will halt from 12-45 pm to 1-30 pm for dinners.

10. 2/Lt Scott and 8 men Hq Coy will act as rear party, and will ensure that all billets are left scrupulously clean, and will without fail obtain clearing certificate from the Town Mayor - this will be handed in to Orderly Room immediately on arrival in new station.
This party will join the Battalion at new station after obtaining clearing certificate.

11. OC Coys will render to Orderly Room by 7 am certificate that billets have been left scrupulously clean.

W.F. Luckman
Captain a/ajt
2/6 Bn. Duke of Wellington's Regt.

Issued at 9 pm

Copy No 1. CO   No 8. P.M.   No 11. R.S.M.
2-6. Coys & Sqn.   9. Adjt.   12. Retain.
7. T.O.   10. 2/Lt Scott   13-14. War Diary.

2/6. BN. DUKE OF WELLINGTON'S (W.R.) Regt.   20.12.1917
ANNEXE TO BATN. ORDER NO. 71

The u/m. have been awarded the MILITARY MEDAL.

266356. Pte. ROBERT STEVENS :— For conspicuous bravery & coolness in carrying out his duties as Battalion runner during the operations against the HINDENBURG Support Line and BOURLON between Nov. 20th & Nov. 28th 1917. He frequently carried messages through heavy hostile & machine gun fire. On Nov. 28th he was despatched with a message from Bn H.Qrs. to a Company in the vicinity of BOURLON WOOD. Though wounded he pushed on, delivered his message, & returned with an answer before having his wound dressed.

267272. Cpl. MICHAEL EGAN :— For great courage & total disregard of danger on the morning of Nov. 27th 1917 during the attack on BOURLON VILLAGE. When enemy snipers & machine gunners were causing heavy casualties to his Company he took a Lewis gun into a building in BOURLON & established himself at a window where two men had already been killed. Though only a short distance from the enemy & subject to their rifle fire he continued to operate the Lewis gun till the party of the enemy which was opposing his C/S were killed or dispersed.

265664. Cpl. CHRISTOPHER METCALFE :— For courage, coolness & devotion to duty in conducting the ration Convoy on Nov. 27th 1917 to the Battalion who were engaged in operations in BOURLON WOOD. This work was performed under heavy & continuous shell fire and he set a splendid example to the men by his coolness & courage. On another occasion, at HERMIES on the 3rd Dec 17, when the horse lines were being shelled by the enemy this N.C.O. again showed remarkable courage in getting the wounded away & assisting in moving the horses to a place of safety.

265690. Sgt. RICHARD MASON :— For marked courage & initiative during the operations Nov. 26th & 28th 1917 in BOURLON WOOD. This N.C.O. who was in charge of the Battn Signal Section continued throughout this period to maintain signal communication under very heavy artillery & M.G. fire. By organising visual stations when his telephone lines were destroyed beyond repair he maintained communication throughout the operations.

266951. L/Cpl RICHARD NOTTER :— For courage & initiative on Nov. 28th 17. during the attack between ANNEUX & BOURLON WOOD. This N.C.O. was in charge of a Lewis Gun team on the right flank of his Company. Heavy casualties were being caused by a party of the enemy firing from the direction of ANNEUX. Without waiting for orders L/Cpl NOTTER crept forward under rifle & M.G. fire to a commanding position & opened fire with his Lewis Gun on the enemy, killing several & dispersing the rest of the party.

W.J. Luckman
Captain & Adjutant,
2/6. BN. DUKE OF WELLINGTON'S (WEST RIDING) REGIMENT.

(2) ANNEXE to 2/6 BN. DUKE OF WELLINGTON'S (W.R.) REGT. ORDER NO. 71 of 20.12.1917.

The after have been awarded the MILITARY MEDAL.

266956 Cpl. WILLIAM CATON:- For conspicuous bravery on Nov. 20th 1917 during the attack on the HINDENBURG Support Line & HUGHES SWITCH. A hostile trench mortar was in action from a point slightly in advance of HUGHES SWITCH. This NCO rushed forward and bayonetted the men in charge of the trench mortar & took prisoner an officer & 8 men who emerged from a dugout close at hand.

267043 Pte. SAMUEL HODGES:- For great dash & bravery on Nov. 27th 1917 during the attack on BOURLON Village. This man is a No.1 Lewis gunner took up a position in a house on the right of the BN's objective in the main street of the village. The enemy delivered a strong counter-attack against this point; Pte. HODGES continued to fire his Lewis Gun with great effect until the enemy were within a few yards of his position. Being almost entirely unsupported he withdrew through a window in rear of the house to high ground slightly in rear from which he re-opened fire on the advancing enemy, thus contributing largely to the repulsion of the hostile attack.

266022 L/Cpl. JOSEPH PATTISON:- For coolness & courage in conducting Ration Convoy on Nov. 28th 1917 to the Battn. who were engaged in Operations in BOURLON WOOD. This work was performed under heavy & continuous shell fire & he set a splendid example to the men. On another occasion he volunteered to go to GRAINCOURT on the 29 Nov. 17 & conducted a G.S. wagon to recover the body of an officer who had been killed, and, although under heavy shell fire conducted the party to the place appointed & showed great courage & determination.

300099 Pte. ALFRED STANDISH:- For great courage and devotion to duty during the attack on the HINDENBURG Support System near GRAINCOURT on Nov. 20th & 21st 1917. This man acted as runner & was on duty continuously for 2 days & 1 night with his Company, often taking messages under M.G. fire to Platoons in the front line, thereby keeping his Coy. Commander in constant touch with events.

240661 Sgt. WILLIAM DAVIES:- For dash & good leadership on Nov. 21st 17 when holding a part of the newly won line in front of BOURLON WOOD which was temporarily out of touch with BTN. on the left. The enemy tried to turn the flank by a bombing attack & this NCO immediately took charge of the nearest Platoon (not his own) & cleared the trench, himself leading the attack.

11636. Pte. FRANCIS DEVANNIE:- For great bravery & resolution whilst acting as Coy. runner during the operations near the HINDENBURG Support Line on Nov. 20th. Throughout the day under heavy fire he continued to carry messages to & from BN. H.Qrs. & to Companies on the flanks. He set a fine example of devotion to duty & showed a complete disregard for his own safety.

W.J. Luckman Captain & Adjutant
2/6 BN. DUKE OF WELLINGTON'S (WEST RIDING) REGIMENT.

(3). ANNEXEE TO 2/6. BN. DUKE OF WELLINGTONS (W.R.) REGT. ORDER No 71 of 20.12.1917.

The u/m have been awarded the MILITARY MEDAL.

265828. Cpl. GEORGE BOWMAN :- For initiative and devotion to duty during the engagement on Novr 27th 1917. After the officer and sergeant of his Platoon had become casualties he took command and gallantly led his Platoon under heavy hostile Machine Gun fire through difficult country in BOURLON WOOD, to its final objective. Afterwards, realising that he was the senior N.C.O, he rendered invaluable assistance in reorganising the Company and holding the men together.

267279. Pte. HERBERT COOKE :- For courage and dash on Novr 27th 1917, during the attack in BOURLON WOOD. A party of the enemy which had escaped our barrage, opened rifle fire on our advancing troops, causing several casualties. This man rushed forward at great personal risk, and himself shot three of the party. His action caused the remainder of the enemy to disperse.

266766. Pte. ALBERT VICTOR ROBINSON :- For bravery and coolness on Novr 21st 1917, during the attack on the HINDENBURG SUPPORT LINE, North of the CAMBRAI ROAD. When his Company was temporarily held up by Machine Gun fire from the front, and its flank threatened by a strong enemy bombing party, this man took up a position in the open in front of the German wire, and continued (under heavy fire) firing rifle grenades until incapacitated by wounds. His gallant action frustrated the attempt to turn the flank of his Company.

265835. Sgt. ARTHUR SMITH :- For courage and initiative during the attack on the HINDENBURG SUPPORT LINE on Novr 20th 1917. This N.C.O was acting as C.S.M and when he saw the Company held up by Machine Gun fire, without further orders, himself led forward a party of men under very heavy fire to the flank of the hostile M.G position, whence he was able to bring sufficient fire onto the machine gunners to make it possible for his Company to advance. Throughout the operations his coolness, disregard of danger, and unfailing cheerfulness was an inspiration to others.

Edw C Cole Lt.
for Captain & Adjutant.
2/6. BN. DUKE OF WELLINGTONS (WEST RIDING) REGIMENT.

(4) ANNEXEE to 2/6th BN. DUKE OF WELLINGTON'S (W.R.) REGT. ORDER NO. 71 of 20.12.17.

The u/m have been awarded the MILITARY MEDAL.

266966. Pte. ROBERT BATESON :- For total disregard of danger and devotion to duty whilst acting as Stretcher-Bearer during the attack on the HINDENBURG SUPPORT SYSTEM near GRAINCOURT on Novr 20th & 21st 1917. He dressed wounds and got back casualties during the whole of Novr 20th under Machine Gun fire, and went out alone on Novr 21st and brought in a badly wounded man from the front of the forward line, thereby undoubtedly saving his life.

266403. L/Cpl. ALFRED CAREY :- For great dash and gallantry. Early in the engagement in BOURLON WOOD on Novr 27th 1917, he gallantly dashed forward with his Lewis Gun, took up a position and put out of action an enemy Machine Gun which was causing us great casualties and holding up our advance.

267212. Pte. BENJAMIN KNOTT SIMPSON :- During the engagement in BOURLON WOOD on Novr 27th 1917, he gallantly left a good position with his Lewis Gun, to take up one nearer the enemy from whence he could cover our advance to the German line. He kept his Gun working under very heavy hostile Machine Gun and rifle fire.

10921. L/Sgt. GEORGE RIGG :- For devotion to duty and courage, during the attack on BOURLON village on Novr 27th 1917. When his Platoon had reached their objective in the village, this N.C.O. rendered valuable assistance in organising the position for defence. He twice went to the unit on the flank for some ammunition. The position became almost surrounded by the enemy. At this stage L/Sgt Rigg with his men continued rapid fire, until the officer in charge gave the order to withdraw to a position about 150 yards in rear.

269304. Pte. WILL. HENRY MOKES :- For remarkable courage and marked bravery while acting as Company Runner during the assault on BOURLON, on Novr 27th & 28th 1917. During this period, this man continued carrying messages and acting as a guide under very heavy shell and Machine Gun fire.

Edw C Cole Lt.
for Captain and Adjutant
2/6th BN. DUKE OF WELLINGTONS (WEST RIDING) REGIMENT.

(3) ANNEXE TO 2/6TH DUKE OF WELLINGTON'S (W.R.) REGT. ORDER NO. 71 d 20.12.17

The following have been awarded the MILITARY MEDAL.

266926 Sgt. THOMAS HENRY GARVEY :- For great endurance and devotion to duty, especially during the attack on POELCAPELLE against the ANTWERPEN strong point, when the supply of S.A.A. was running short. This N.C.O. made several journeys to and from BATTN. H.Q. to BATTALION Dump, carrying over heavy shelled areas, and brought back supplies of ammunition.

28099? L/Cpl. JAMES MIDGLEY :- For great bravery and initiative on Nov. 20th 1917, during the attack on the HINDENBURG SUPPORT. When the Company was temporarily held up by severe machine gun fire from both flanks he took out a Lewis Gun to the left flank of the Company, and though under heavy m.g. and howe fire, engaged the enemy behind him with direct fire, and thus enabled his Company to advance.

Edw C. Cole. Lt.
for — Captain & Adjutant
2/6th Bn. Duke of Wellington's (West Riding) Regiment

12.V.
22 sheets

War Diary

of

2/6th Bn. Duke of Wellingtons Rgt.

from January 1st 1918. to January 31st 1918.

Volume 12

L.S. Rimble Lt. Col.
O.C. 2/6 Bn. Duke of Wellington Rgt.

ORIGINAL

Army Form C. 2118.

WAR DIARY 2/6 DUKE OF WELLINGTONS
or
INTELLIGENCE SUMMARY. (W.R.) REGT
(Erase heading not required.)

Instructions regarding War Diaries and Intelligence Summaries are contained in F.S. Regs., Part II. and the Staff Manual respectively. Title pages will be prepared in manuscript.

Place	Date	Hour	Summary of Events and Information	Remarks and references to Appendices
	1/18			
LENS?	Jan. 1		The Batt. marched from VILLERS BRULIN to SAVY + entrained. On arriving at ARRAS the Batt. detrained + marched to AUBREY CAMP. G.H.Q.2.S. Sheet 51.B. E.C. Camp was taken over from the 1/13 LONDON REGT (QUEEN VICTORIA RIFLES) 58 Division. Lewis Guns + Q.M. Stores on ST. CATHERINE. Major H.O England rejoined the Batt.	Sigs
AUBREY CAMP G.H.Q.2.S Sheet 51.B.	2	9-12½	Training. 1220 carried out. 200 Haversacks + 200 Waterbottles indented N.S.	Sigs
		2 PM	Football Match 1/13 LONDON REGT (KENSINGTON RIFLES) 1 goal 2/6 DUKE OF WELLINGTONS NIL	Sigs
	3		The Batt. supplied working parties for work in forward areas under R.E.	Sigs
	4		" "	R.V.
	5		Practice Platoon in attack	Sig
	6		" "	Sig
			The Batt. supplied working parties for work in forward area under R.E.	
			The following were mentioned for meritorious service during the recent offensive operations 30/9/17	
			2Lt A.T. Allander (K/A) Capt F.R. Nelson R.A.M.C. Rev. H.R. Jagger C.F. 285720. 2S.M. Clarken N. 266283. L/Cpl Oliking. G. 300060. A/Cpl Smith H. 25115. C/L Maggatt. H. 266357. L/Cpl Hook Q.	Sigs
	7		The Batt. carried out training	Sigs
	8		" " supplied parties for work in the forward area under 573 Coy R.E.	Sigs
	9		The Batt. marched to ANZIN	Sigs

ORIGINAL.

WAR DIARY
or
INTELLIGENCE SUMMARY.
(Erase heading not required.)

2/6 DUKE OF WELLINGTONS (W.R.) REGT.

Army Form C. 2118.

Place	Date	Hour	Summary of Events and Information	Remarks and references to Appendices
SPECIAL MAP	JAN 10		The Batt. relieved the 1/9 (Q.V.R.) LONDON REGT. in the RED LINE. B + D Coys	
FOOT HILL 1/20.000			Billets to BIYEH. A + C. Coys at DITCH POST B.23.d. Batt HQrs at B.23.a.2.6	
	11	AM 30PM	Working parties at night dug Cable trench under Corps. supervision	SwS
			Working parties worked under direction of 457 Coy R.E in the Corps Main System	
	12	MIDNIGHT	until 12 midnight . Platoon won the Brigade Tactical exercise	1st Sgt
		4.30 PM	Parties worked under 457 Coy. R.E on Corps Main System until 12.30 A.M.	Sgt
	13		" " " "	
51 B N.W	14		The batt. was relieved by the 2/5 Y + L. Regt. HQrs. A + C. Coys went to	
			NIC + B + D. Coys to WAKEFIELD CAMP when Billets were taken over	Sgt...
			from 2/5 K.O.Y.L.I. The batt: was in Brigade Reserve.	Sgt
	15		Parties were found to work in the forward area	Sgt
	16		" " " " " " "	
	17		" " " " " By the C.O + 1/c Coys	
			Marked the Line.	
	18		The Batt: relieved the 2/4 DUKE OF WELLINGTONS in the line in INVRELLE Area	W.S.
			+ held MILL POST. G.19.a + c. Batt HQrs at B.30.a. B.9.	

WAR DIARY
or
INTELLIGENCE SUMMARY.

Army Form C. 2118.

2/6 DUKE OF WELLINGTON'S (W.R) REGT.

Place	Date	Hour	Summary of Events and Information	Remarks and references to Appendices
	1916			
S1.B.N.W.	JAN 19		The trenches are in a very bad condition owing to the recent frost + rain.	S47
			Enemy movement very quiet. One of their trenches seen in a bad condition.	S47
			Both our + enemy planes doing recon. 3 German planes seen.	S47
	20		FRESNEY rationally unknown.	S47
			Enemy movement has been the same.	"
			Unusually quiet. Enemy trench mortars and rifle grenades firing.	S47
	21		do. morning	
			The usual aerial activity was observed. Grenades 1 killed, 3 wounded.	S47
	22		The Batt. was relieved by the 2/4 Y. & L. Regt. + went into billets at MARŒUIL as Div. Reserve. Relief complete 9.30 P.M.	S47
	23		The day was spent in cleaning up. Kit inspections.	S47
	24		A party of 4 who furnished fy. work in the forward area.	S47
	25		Specialist training.	S47
	26		- do -	S47
	27		A party was provided for work in the forward area. Church Parade for Divine Service in Y.M.C.A. tent.	S47
	28			S47

ORIGINAL

WAR DIARY
or
INTELLIGENCE SUMMARY.

Army Form C. 2118.

2/6 DUKE OF WELLINGTONS (W.R.) REGT

(Erase heading not required.)

Place	Date	Hour	Summary of Events and Information	Remarks and references to Appendices
	1918			
51 B N W.	Jan 28	8:30 pm	A supper was given to No 13 Platoon (the winners of the Brigade Football Competition Scheme) & H.Q. Coy Football team (winners B Batt League). Speeches were made by the C.O. & Major England & were replied to by 2 Rail Kirk.	Sur 1. Cur 1.
	29	11:30 am	Major Gen. R. Benthwork CB inspected the hutts & presented ribbons to the N.C.Os & Men who were awarded the Military Medal for acts of gallantry at CAMBRAI.	M.M.
		8:30 am	The Sgts held a smoking concert. Speeches were made by the CO & Major England & Capt Singh C.F. Mention of the discharge of the late Sgt was made.	Curt.
	30		Arrangements made for the breaking up of the Batt	Sur.
	31		At 10 am the Batt. paraded for the last time & the men interested by the C.O. The whole Batt. were then split into three parties & were marched off to join the 5th, the 7th & the 2/7th Bn. D. of W's (W.R.) Regt respectively, under the reorganisation scheme by which brigades consist of 9 instead of 12 Batts.	Sur.

Army Form C. 2118.

WAR DIARY
or
INTELLIGENCE SUMMARY.
(Erase heading not required.)

2/6 Bn. Duke of Wellington's (W.R.) Regt.

Instructions regarding War Diaries and Intelligence Summaries are contained in F.S. Regs., Part II. and the Staff Manual respectively. Title pages will be prepared in manuscript.

Place	Date	Hour	Summary of Events and Information	Remarks and references to Appendices
	1918			
S713 NW	Jan 31		NOTE BY C.O.	
			The breaking up of the Battalion is greatly deplored by all ranks, but the knowledge that it is disbanding for the consolidation & common benefit of the Regiment serving in the XII Corps mitigates to some extent the regret of all concerned. Every Officer, Warrant Officer, N.C.O. & man leaves the Battalion actuated by a desire & strong determination to carry with them into their new units the enthusiasm, loyalty, they have ever displayed for the King, Country, Regiment & above all the abiding principles & spirit of Esprit de Corps which have always been so well established in the 2/6 Battalion, Duke of Wellington's (West Riding) Regiment.	
			GOD SAVE THE KING.	
			R.S. Crawley M.Cl.	
			Cmdg 2/6 Bn. D. of W. (W.R.) Regt.	

2/6. BN. DUKE OF WELLINGTON'S REGT.   Copy No. 7
       OPERATION   ORDER NO. 51.

Refce LENS. 11. 1/100.000.   8 JANY. 1917.

1. The Battalion will move by march route to Billets at ANZIN tomorrow.

2. INSTRUCTIONS.
   (a) **Order of march:**– H.Qrs. A. B. C. D.
       Dress:– Marching Order with 1 blanket. Jerkins will be worn.
   (b) **Starting point:**– 56th Divnl. Church on ARRAS ROAD.
   (c) **Route**   :– via ST. CATHERINE.
   (d) **Time**   :– H.Qrs. to pass starting point at 11. a.m.
   (e) **Intervals** :– 200x interval will be maintained between Coys.
   (f) Coys. will parade independently and march off in the proper order.
       Care should be taken not to keep men on parade longer than necessary.
   (g) **Transport** : 1 limber for Lewis Gun &c. will accompany each Coy.
                        and 1 for HQrs.
                        The Mess Cart, 2 Water Carts & 4 Field Kitchens
                        will accompany the Battalion. The Maltese Cart
                        will not go with the Bn. The M.O. will arrange
                        for 1 pannier & 2 stretchers to be loaded with
                        H.Qrs. limber.

   (h) **Advanced parties:**–
            Advanced parties as arranged will report to 2/LT. THOMPSON at
       the Orderly Room at 9.am tomorrow and will take over billets for their
       Coys. and H.Qrs.
   (i) **Coy. Stores.**
            Will be stored in the Canteen Hut, being divided into 2
       parts – those wanted in the RED LINE & those not wanted.
   (j) **Rear Parties.**
            Each Coy. and H.Qrs. will leave behind 1.N.C.O. and
       2 (or 3) Pte. to clean up the camp, help load stores &c as required
       and later to accompany the limbers taking stores &c. to the
       RED LINE in the afternoon. They will take over accommodation
       in that line on behalf of their Coys. &c. and remain there until
       the arrival of the Battalion.
            In addition, O.C. B Coy. will detail 1.N.C.O. and 6 men for
       loading blankets. These will proceed to ANZIN with them.
   (k) **Blankets &c.**
            Transport for these will be provided by Bde. Details later.
   (l) Dinners will be cooked during the march & served at ANZIN.

                                            E. W. Taylor
                                                               Lieut. Jady.
Issued at 8.45 p.m.   2/6. BN. DUKE OF WELLINGTON'S (W.R.) REGT.

Copy No. 1. Retained   Copy No. 9. Q.M.
        2. C.O. ✓   10. T.O.
        3. Adj.   11 ⎫ War Diary
        4–8 Coys & HQrs.   12 ⎭

www.ingramcontent.com/pod-product-compliance
Lightning Source LLC
Chambersburg PA
CBHW081425160426
43193CB00013B/2192